HANDMADE PAPER

About the Editor

The Editor of this book is himself a champion of Village Industries. He believes in service and pleads to get Financial and Technological inputs to the Village Industries Sector. Handmade paper is an area of his special interest. He has developed some concepts for promotion of Handmade Paper Industries. As Chairman, Khadi and Village Industries Commission, he introduced numerous things to expand Village Industries. Cylinder mould was introduced during his tenure. He takes keen interest in developing and marketing of Village Industries products and specially Handmade Paper. As a result Handmade Paper Industry took fast pace during his tenure as Chairman, Khadi and Village Industries Commission.

Handmade Paper

From Rags to Riches

Edited by

Laxmi Dass

AKHIL BHARTIYA GRAMODHYOG MAHASANGH

and

CONCEPT PUBLISHING COMPANY, NEW DELHI-110059

ISBN 13: 978-81-8069-530-8 **ISBN 10: 81-8069-530-1**

First Published 2009

Published and Printed by

Concept
Since 1974

Concept Publishing Company
Regd. Office:
A/15-16, Commercial Block, Mohan Garden
New Delhi-110059 (India)
Phones : 25351460, 25351794, *Fax* : 091-11-25357109
Email : publishing@conceptpub.com,
website: www.conceptpub.com

Editorial Office:
H-13, Bali Nagar, New Delhi-110 015, India.

Cataloging in Publication Data--*Courtesy:* D.K. Agencies (P) Ltd. <docinfo@dkagencies.com>

Handmade paper : from rags to riches / edited by Laxmi Dass.
p. cm.
Contributed articles.
In Indian context.
Includes bibliographical references.
Includes index.
ISBN 13: 9788180695308 ISBN 10: 8180695301

1. Paper, Handmade--India--History. 2. Paper industry--Technological innovations--India. I. Dass, Laxmi.

DDC 676.0954 22

Preface

Sufficient Literature has been published for promotion and expansion of Handmade Paper Industries. But there was a great need of a book which gives the complete information of Handmade Paper Industries since its inception. Now-a-days those who are active in the particular field have little time to spare for preparing articles or writing books. I have been toying with the idea to approach some experts who can write on Handmade Paper. While in the process, a National Seminar, conducted for Handmade Paper Industry came in Handy for me. Some experts were requested to prepare papers of their interest in the promotion of Handmade Paper. Some of the experts responded positively, prepared articles and those efforts resulted in the shape of this book. It is very difficult to claim that this book is a complete document for Handmade Paper. But all efforts have been made to cover various areas concerning Handmade Paper. The article writers have put-in their best to prepare these articles. Therefore, it can be said that this is the best book available on Handmade Paper.

Readers will find it, interesting and full of information on different aspects of Handmade Paper. I am sure that these efforts will help those who have even a little interest in Handmade Paper Industry. I congratulate the writers for enriching this document with their expertise. This book in your hands will give a sense of satisfaction to the Editor.

Contents

List of Contributors

Agarwal, Saakshy, Research Assistant, Kumarappa National Handmade Paper Institute, Sanganer, Jaipur.

Atul Kumar, Senior Research Assistant, Kumarappa National Handmade Paper Institute, Sanganer, Jaipur.

Chauhan, Sunita, Research Assistant (Biotech), Kumarappa National Handmade Paper Institute, Sanganer, Jaipur.

Dass, Lakshmi, Ex-Chairman KVIC.

Garg, Pramod, President of All India Handmade Paper Industry Association, General Secretary of Akhil Bhartiya Gramodhyog Mahasangh, Shakarpur, Delhi, Secretary of Shankar Gramodhyog Sewa Sansthan.

Ghosh, G.K., presently Joint CEO, KVIC, has written dozens of books on various subjects. By profession he is a Scientist and a Literary figure.

Jain, R.K., Director, Kumarappa National Handmade Paper Institute, Sanganer, Jaipur.

Khan, Mohd. Esa, Senior Research Assistant, Kumarappa National Handmade Paper Institute, Sanganer, Jaipur.

Pant, Rajesh, Ex-Director, Kumarappa National Handmade Paper Institute, Sanganer, Jaipur.

Prasad, Baleshwer, Pilot Plant Incharge, Kumarappa National Handmade Paper Institute, Sanganer, Jaipur.

Raju, D.S.R., Chief Executive, Green Gallery, New Delhi.

Roy, N.K., Ex-Deputy CEO, KVIC.

Sadique, M., Assistant Director, KVIC.

Sharan, A.K., Deputy Director, KVIC (Khadi and Village Industries Commission).

Sharma, A.K., Deputy Director, Kumarappa National Handmade Paper Institute, Sanganer, Jaipur.

Vijay Kumar, Col. (Retd.) Chief Advisor, All India Handmade Paper Industries Association.

1

Vision 2020

LAXMI DASS

Introduction

Paper is a vehicle on which modern civilization moves. Its use in communications, information industry, education, science and technology is well established.

Handmade paper is a layer of entwined fibres, held together by the natural internal bonding properties of cellulose fibres in the form of diluted pulp lifted by hand.

Per capita consumption of paper, which is an index of educational, industrial and socio-economic development of a country, is around 5.5 kgs in India as compared with 300 to 800 kgs in developed countries like the USA, Canada and Japan, etc. With the growth of literacy and industrialization, per capita consumption of paper/board is bound to increase.

Handmade paper manufacturing is one of the traditional industries of the world. Since its invention in China in 105 A.D. However, Indians are credited to have used paper made from cellulose fibres even during third century B.C. Prior to this, leaves of palm trees were the medium of writing in India while 'papers', made from similar named reed that grew on the banks of the Nile, in Egypt was stated to have been the medium of communication in Egypt.

The handmade paper indstry flourished in India during the Mughal period but gradually declined with the establishment of paper mills during the 18th and 19th centuries. It is noteworthy that the art of handmade paper making was revived under the inspiration of Mahatma Gandhi, the Father of the Nation, during the freedom movement.

After its establishment in 1956, the Khadi and Village Industries Commission, which was constituted under an Act of Parliament, took over the responsibility of revival of village industries, including handmade paper, by way of financing, developing and disseminating technical know-how and lending marketing assistance. Earlier, the industry was being financed under the "pattern system" which provided limited funds for capital expenditure and working capital. To overcome the shortage of funds for assistance, the system was changed to project approach, enabling eligible Village Industry institutions to avail of assistance of up to Rs. 25 lakh and individuals up to Rs. 10 lakh by contributing 10 per cent of the project cost as their share. The system was made applicable to State Khadi and Village Industries Boards also. Financial, technological and marketing assistance extended to this industry by the Khadi and Village Industries Commission over the last four decades has thus not only helped it grow in India but also make its impact felt in the developed countries through export of drawing paper and other items over the last two decades.

Performance of the Industry

In 1953-54, when the All India Khadi and Village Industries Board took up revival of the handmade paper industry, there were only 40 units with annual production of about Rs. 5 lakh. Today, after 46 years of sustained efforts, the industry with its about 3000 working units, has achieved production of paper and converted items valued at Rs. 80.54 crore. The industry now provides gainful employment to around 24,000 persons. Wages earned by these workers are to the tune of Rs. 22 crore, which directly and mainly benefit rural artisans. The salient features of this growth are summarised in Table 1.1:

Table 1.1: Growth of Handmade Paper Industry in India

Year	*No. of Working Units*	*Production (Rs. lakh)*	*Sales (Rs. lakh)*	*Employment (thousand persons)*	*Wages (Rs. lakh)*
1953-54	40	5.00	5.00	1.00	1.70
1960-61	108	24.00	21.00	4.00	9.10
1965-66	149	39.00	36.00	5.00	14.43
1971-72	176	81.00	87.00	4.00	26.24
1976-77	201	156.00	171.00	4.00	51.41
1985-86	251	439.17	463.01	5.00	193.57
1989-90	300	723.76	748.62	5.00	193.57
1990-91	325	852.61	920.64	6.00	256.40
1991-92	344	1210.39	1238.52	7.00	336.89
1992-93	350	1532.12	1604.91	7.50	426.37
1993-94	1246	221.92	2401.82	10.00	624.93
1994-95	1191	3027.45	3325.88	12.00	798.83
1995-96	2293	3511.25	3872.75	15.00	998.22
1996-97	2794	4312.97	4977.65	15.00	1311.22
1997-98	2794	4886.12	5782.77	17.00	1449.97
1998-99	2975	5456.00	6391.76	18.00	1594.98
1999-2000	2616	5821.11	6869.51	19.00	1649.15
2000-01	2750	7322.00	9405.00	22.00	1890.00
2001-02	3000	8054.00	10345.00	24.00	2200.00

Note:
- Paper conversion units were also included from the year 1993-94.
- Female employment is about 35 per cent of the total employment.

The performance of the industry is expected to improve, as more educated people are attracted to the use of handmade paper and also come forward to establish production units or deal in these products.

SWOT Analysis of Handmade Paper Industry

Table 1.2 attempts a "strengths, weaknesses, opportunities and threats" (SWOT) analysis of the industry:

Table 1.2: SWOT Analysis of Handmade Paper Industry

Strengths	*Weaknesses*
• Low per capita investment. • High employment generation. • High percentage of wages. • Use of non-forest raw materials. • Environment-friendly and pollution-free indegenous machinery. • High permanence value and strength of products. • Negligible or no chemical action of the fiber properties. • Low management cost. • Fancy and aesthetic products at affordable cost. • Large scope of producing diversified and value-added products, fetching lucrative returns.	• Lack of professional skills among implementing agencies. • Poor quality control measures. • Dearth of skilled workers. • Inadequate R&D programme. • Absence of aggressive marketing strategies and structures based on modern concepts. • Inordinate delays in commissioning of plants.
Opportunities	*Threats*
• Liberal finance from KVIC, KVIBs, Nationalized banks, etc. • Low cost consultancy and technical know-how from implementing agencies. • Reservation and/or purchase preference in Government procurements. • Raw material support from Government Departments. • Training facilities from KVIC. • Availability of new possible raw materials like barks and jute. • Marketing assistance from KVIC/other Government organisations.	• Decreasing availability of conventional raw materials. • Low per capita consumption of paper in the country. • Imitation of patterns and products by the mill sector. • Applications of labour laws. • Strong lobby against the sector by vested interests.

Demand Projections

According to the Annual Report of 2002-03 of KVIC, handmade paper production in India was about 25,000 MT, which included that of units with registration certificates from and aided by the KVIC/KVIBs and paper board making units but excluded those handmade paper (HMP) units which are not covered under the purview of KVIC.

Reliable data on marketing of HMP products are not available. There is need of product-wise marketing information, in order to identify the approximate products for domestic and global markets. As per information received from the Department of Commerce, Government of India, the export, including HMP and HMP boards during 2002-03 was 10,130/033 kg. However, in the details of export of different types of HMP products, the export data of conventional and fancy items are not available.

Under the circumstances, it is difficult to work out specifics. Based on the feedbacks and estimates of traders and production units it would appear that the demand of HMP products of common use and fancy items as well as file covers and file boards in use of Government Departments is increasing.

It has also been reported that European and other foreign countries have started producing HMP products.

With these broad indicators, it can be inferred that the per capita consumption of paper is on the rise, which is also linked with increasing literacy rate. Although the bulk of this increase is in the demand for mill paper, which is more cost effective, the positive trends in demand for HMP cannot be overlooked.

If HMP units upgrade quality to meet the market requirements, their market share can increase correspondingly. Assuming 3 per cent rise per year, the demand for HMP products, including boards can rise to 40,000 metric tonnes by 2020.

Raw Material

The main raw materials for producing HMP are:

- Cotton Rags
- Sisal Fibre

- Banana Fibre
- Sabai Grass
- Jute Fibre
- Straw
- Sun hemp
- Other Cellulosic Fibre

Currently, 80 to 90 per cent of the raw material used by the HMP industry consists of cotton rags with a small proportion of other raw material. It has been reported that textile mills are increasing the synthetic content in multi fibre products because of their interpretation of the textile policy. However, 100 per cent cotton clothing is being produced, particularly for textile exports. Using the rags from such textile mills will create problems because of the presence of synthetic fiber. The problem needs to be addressed. Technology intervention at this level will improve the quality of Handmade Paper products.

Experiments with Alternative Raw Materials

Currently, the handmade paper units use cotton rags for manufacturing paper. Banana fibre is also being used to make specialized paper and some efforts have been made to convert other fibres as raw material for handmade paper. But all these efforts are still at laboratory level. The availability of cotton rags is coming down while the demand is increasing. Therefore, other fibres, which have the property to enable their use as raw materials for handmade paper, need to be promoted.

The Research and Development Institute for HMP, *i.e.*, Science and Technology Projects on Handmade Paper at Forest Institute, Dehradun, different individual units recognized by KVIC, Handmade Paper Institute, Pune and KNHPI (Kumarappa National Handmade Paper Institute, Jaipur) have worked on the following alternative raw materials and the results are encouraging. The products made of different raw materials are as under:

Aak (Calotropis)	Tissue paper of high strength and transparency; similar to Chinese xen paper.
Banana	Tissue paper, paper for conservation of old and fragile documents, lamp shade papers, gift wraps and different types of export variety paper.
Jute	Suitable raw material to make card sheets, file covers and high strength carry bag paper.
Rice and wheat straw	Boards and packing varieties of paper.
Mulberry	Lightweight, transparent paper similar to Thai paper.
Ambadi	Card paper and cover paper.

Trials have been conducted by IIT, Roorkee, NIT (National Institute of Technology), Rourkela, KNHPI, Jaipur and HMP Institute, Pune on all the above-mentioned fibers. If HMP units come forward, these experiments/trials may lead to wider and commercial use of other raw materials for HMP.

Value Addition and Product Diversification

The various value added products of handmade paper have ample demand in the national and international markets. The upward trend noticed during the last ten years in demand for value added products is growing consistently.

Vision 2020

The Vision that we envisage for the handmade paper industry is summarised under the following headings:

Technology

- By the year 2020, new technology suitable to the HMP shall be developed. In certain areas existing technology shall be upgraded to suit the growth of this industry and some downsized mill technology may be inducted. Quality upgradation shall be the major thrusts.

- Machines for making more uniform sheets with higher efficiency, productivity and operational ease will replace the existing papermaking vats or dipping or cylinder mould vats.
- More economical and affordable drying systems, including those using non-conventional energy like solar, wind and biomass, will become available.
- Instead of covering large areas, multi storyed buildings will be the preference of handmade paper units.
- More energy efficient machines, for example, beaters, shall be designed.
- A super calendar or calendaring machine suitale to ensure the quality of handmade paper shall be introduced.
- R&D shall be the major thrust and continous process in the years to come.
- As it appears, water scarcity will be a major problem, not only for India but also the whole of the world. Technology shall be developed to re-use process water in the industry.
- Quality control laboratories will be set up region-wise and, later, unit-wise. Almost each production unit would prefer to have quality control laboratory to ensure quality for the paper.

Value Addition

- Value addition shall become the major priority of the industry.
- More and more traditional and non-traditional artisans will adopt conversion of handmade paper as their career. More and more entrepreneurs, artisans and converters will get opportunity to prove their skills and innovative ideas.
- The additions to existing product range will increase in multiple ways.
- Suitable paper will be developed for use with computers and such other areas where handmade paper is not found suitable today.

Raw Material

- The imbalance between demand and supply of cotton rags will compel the entrepreneurs and the scientists to look for alternative or additional raw materials for handmade paper.
- Different types of fibres available in different parts of the country will find greater use.
- No fiber shall be allowed to go waste but converted into wealth.
- The researchers, scientists and entrepreneurs shall take up experiments on one fiber and on combination of fibers in varying ratios.
- Recycling of papers will take place in a big way. No used paper shall be wasted.
- Techniques shall be developed to segregate the synthetic rags from cotton rags and for decolourization of cotton rags to suit the industry.

Marketing

- There shall be aggressive marketing of handmade paper and its products.
- Product launching system shall be adopted to give boost to the marketing of handmade paper.
- Marketing campaigns at local, district, state, national and international levels shall be a continuous process.
- New clientele shall be found, new users shall be developed, virgin areas shall be looked into and keeping the demands of new and old users in view, handmade paper products shall be developed. It will be both ways, products according to the demand and creation of demand for handmade paper and its products.
- The handmade paper industries will not only look to the niche markets but will also develop affordable products for the common people.

- Workshops, seminars and conferences shall be conducted to improve and popularize handmade paper and its products.
- Looking at the growth potential of handmade paper, its market share will increase ten to twelve folds.
- The demand in the government sector shall be utilized but more and more emphasis shall be given on the consumer market.
- NCERT, CBSE, State Education Boards, Universities and similar organizations will prefer to use handmade paper.
- Latest marketing devices like websites, E-business and other similar systems shall also be utilized by handmade paper industry.
- Regarding exports, the handmade paper industry will make the best use of available resources and facilities. The exports of handmade paper will increase 15 fold by 2020.
- The handmade paper industry shall participate in international exhibitions in a big way.
- There shall be a handmade paper export promotion council to look after its the exports.
- Database for planning the production and marketing of handmade paper shall be updated.

Clusters

- To give boost to the handmade paper industry, clusters/ mother units/service centers shall be established in various parts of the country, to function as raw material banks and training facilities and to upgrade quality and provide marketing support to the handmade paper units.
- These clusters will function as model centers to inspire the unemployed youth to adopt handmade paper industry as their careers.
- These clusters will also help panchayats to earn revenue and promote public private partnership.

- The clusters shall be the focal points for systematic growth of rural industrialization.

Employment Generation

- Unemployment will continue to be a major problem for the country and the society will hunt for avenues of employment generation. The handmade paper industry shall partly answer this question.
- The production of handmade paper is sure to generate employment but the conversion of handmade paper sheets into different useful and customer friendly products will have the major share in employment generation. The employment generation will increase five fold by 2020.

Policy Support

- Government of India shall come out with policy support to promote handmade paper industry.
- The Government of India and the financial institutions will provide liberal financial assistance to establish, promote and expand the handmade paper industry.
- Looking to the growth and utility of handmade paper, particularly with reference to its scope for employment generation, the Government of India will provide fiscal concessions to the industry.
- Handmade paper will become one of the thrust areas to generate employment and Government of India will treat this industry accordingly.

Role of Federations

- The handmade paper industry will organize itself into federations at the district, state and regional levels.
- The national level handmade paper associations shall become a powerful organ to protect, promote and patronize handmade paper at national and international levels.

- A need may arise to have national level marketing association exclusively for handmade paper.
- Federations and associations will take up the job which individual units will not be able to do.

Role of KVIC

- Khadi and Village Industries Commission will continue to be a national body to provide help for the growth of the handmade paper industry and continue to provide financial assistance, skill upgradation, training, technology upgradation and other related support to the handmade paper industry.

Role of Training Institutes

- The training institutes run by the KVIC, KVIBs and other similar institutions will continue to provide training on more professional ways of production and management and will produce entrepreneurs to take-up handmade paper industry.

The Role of R&D Institutions

- The science and technology institutes will make efforts to develop technologies suitable for the growth of handmade paper industry.
- TIFAC and KNHPI, Jaipur will have major responsibility to develop and uprade appropriate technology for the smooth growth of handmade paper industry. These technology-based Institutions will also coordinate the research programmes undertaken by different research centers or IITs.

Conclusion

India will maintain its first position in the international market in respect of handmade paper and handmade paper products.

Target production will be around 91000 tonnes by 2020 with a sales target of Rs. 20040 crore. The employment is expected to increase 92500 through this eco-friendly industry.

Akhil Bhartiya Gramodhyog Mahasangh, in close contact with various government, non-government organisations and handmade paper units will do its best to see the handmade paper industry growing fast and branching out in a big way to contribute to the growth of the country.

2

History of Handmade Paper

G.K. GHOSH

Not only handmade paper but paper in General symbolizes the development of the country. The per capita consumption of paper indicates development status and literary status of the country. Inspite of the fact that has been in use paper since several centuries back, the per capita consumption of paper remains far behind. Other developing countries like Indonesia, Malayasia etc. However the fact remains that paper was not developed in India, it was developed elsewhere.

Historically paper making, to be more specific handmade paper was developed simultaneously in two different countries, Egypt and China. In India the technology entered from China through two different routes. The first was through Mangolian routes due to interaction which entered through Tibet, Nepal and good cluster developed around Darjeeling, Arunachal Pradesh, etc. The second route was through Mughal era where the group of prisoners of war between Mughals and China were resettled around Jaipur to develop the Cluster in Sanganer, few of them known as Kagzis migrated to various other places like Maharashtra and U.P. and developed clusters around. However it is reported that the art of paper making in India started as far back as 3rd century B.C. The clusters found, in all these states are not the alike. As the places like Bhagwangola in Murshidabad District, Dasghara in Hugli District and Maiman in Howrah all in West Bengal besides Junner and Khaltabad in Maharashtra and many other places. During Mughal period all these clusters were known as Kagzipura.

To start with we may mention about the definition of handmade paper as has been defined in the Dictionary of Paper, American Paper and Pulp Association is given below:

"Handmade paper is a layer of entwined fibres, held together by the natural internal bonding properties of cellulose fibres lifted by hand, sheet by sheet on moulds in suspension of fibres in water with or without sizing."

Handmade peper has gone through various stages in technological transformation. It started with traditional, method with exploration. There was improved technology which was further developed by KVIC and finally cylinder mould was developed subsequently to increase the productivity, which is given in the below mentioned paragraphs:

Traditional Method of Handmade Paper Making

During Mughal period the principal raw material was jute gunny bags and waste paper. The gunny bags were cut in small pieces and soaked in lime water for around ten days for softening the fibre and removing the unwanted material, which may tarnish the quality of paper. The original method for beating or macerating the jute gunny bags to pulp by way of placing the material with water in stone mortars and pounding the mass to fiber by means of pastels or mallets operated by hand. This equipment was called Dhenki. During the early hours of the day it could be easily identified by the rhythmic sound of these dhemkies that there is a "Kagzipura" in the near vicinity.

The pulp thus formed was put in wooden vats with measured quantity of water for diluting. This mixture was stirred with a wooden stick for evenly mixing the pulp with water. Grass or Bamboo mats specially made for screening the pulp, which were called chhapris. Both the ends of the chhapris were tied or fixed to wooden rolls or stick to keep the mat in place. These chhapris which were flexible, extended with help of two wooden rods/sticks on the sides and dipped into the vat for lifting a measured quantity of pulp. The excess water of the pulp drains out from the chhapri and a layer of the pulp deposits on the surface of the chhapri which is the wet form of paper. The paper thus formed is pressed on the couching table having piles of cotton cloth pieces along with the mat so that the paper is transferred to the cloth. Thus a pile of such sandwich of paper and cloth is kept overnight under a heavy stone or weight for draining forty-fifty per cent of the water. After draining the water the paper was peeled off from the pile and was pasted along with cloth on the walls coated with lime and the cloth is peeled off slowly without disturbing the formation of paper. These papers were kept for a day for drying.

These papers thus dried were collected and one by one were polished in wooden equipment, which had a base of curved surface, and stone roll, which is burshed on the paper, kept on the curved surface. The paper sheets than collected and the edges were trimmed by knife in exact size of requirement. The paper thus produced were ported to marketplaces in the cities and sold by the kagzis and other vendors.

Introduction of Improved Technology of Handmade Papermaking

This art of handmade papermaking had a set back after the advent of British and almost touched it's nadir. It was the inspiration of Mahatma Gandhi. The Father of Nation who revived the art of a Handmade Paper and rehabilitated the status of kagzis. During this time All India Khadi Gramodhyog Sangh was established (1934) for the up-liftment of cottage industries. Further during 1940 late Shri K.B. Joshi had the idea in his mind for adapting intermediate technology by use of power in certain areas for the improvement of quality and productivity of paper.

Several developments have been experienced after the use of power in the paper-making. The traditional way of rag cutting manually by hand was replaced by the rag chopper. The pulping by dhenki was also replaced by the beater and so on in all the processes except the paper lifting which is done by hand to project the identity of the handmade paper.

In the meanwhile new explorations were occurred in the field of raw material, the usage of gunny/jute, waste paper were slowly diminished and rags came into usage as primary raw material. Also the agrobased raw materials like banana, sunhemp, sabai grass, straw, Daphne etc, came into usage. Inspite all the improvements in the manufacturing of Handmade Paper the basic mechanism of sheet formation is maintained and restricted to manual hand lifting only so as to safe guard the identity of Handmade Paper. The development in formation of the sheet was to pour a measured quantity of pulp to a mould fixed in the deckle inside the vat instead of the traditional method of dipping system.

Intermediate Techcnology of Handmade Paper-making by Cylinder Mould Vat

The sheet formed by dipping method and hand vat needed screw press/hydraulic press. The introduction of Cylinder Mould Vat by way of intermediate technology made the process easier by way of replacing the vat the press (Screw press/ Hydraulic press). Rest of the process remained same. No doubt the quality and quantity of the production increased with introduction of Cylinder Mould Vat. The paper is formed by the depositon of the fibre on the surface of the cylindrical mould with is in the process transferred by the conveyer belt (felt) to a solid cylinder (pin cut roll) where the sheet is removed one by one.

The KVIC adapted the power driven Cylinder Mould Vat (CMV) of maximum 30" face during the year 1988 for avoiding the drudgery of artisans/workers, increasing the productivity improving the quality and to make it more economically viable.

During the year 1990 KVIC had amended the restriction on the face of the CMV from 30" to 40" on a plea from the production units.

On adoption of CMV, KVIC had to make a nominal change in the definition of the handmade paper as *"the paper made from the pulp sheet by sheet."*

To be brief in tabulated form the difference between the traditional process and improved process is given below:

	Traditional Process (Old Process)	*Improved Process (Present Process)*
	Machinery	
I.	Old dhenkies and trampling pits for pulp making.	Power driven beater.
II.	Dipping vats for paper formation.	Mechanically operated vats and Dipping vats, as under Mould vat.
III.	Grass moulds (chhari).	Wire gauge moulds with wooden frame, Nylon, Bamboo Chhapri.
IV.	Heavy weight stones for squeezing out water from paper.	Hand operated screw press and power operated hydraulic press.
V.	Burnished stone for polishing of paper, agata-stone.	Plate glazing calendar machine, power-operated.
VI.	Knife for paper cutting.	Hand or power operated cutting machine.
VII.	Knife for cutting of raw material.	Power operated cuttlers Rag Chopper.
VIII.	Waste paper, old and new cotton rags cutting, old fisherman nets, jute gunny bag.	Old and new rag cuttings, jute and Hussein waste cutting, waste paper, straw and grasses silk thread, wool fur, hair, synthetic fiber, agricultural and forest waste, asbestos, etc.
IX.	Blotting, Writing, Printing, Bahikhata (Account books).	Drawing, bonds documents, certificates, duplicating, gross mottle, marbles, velvet, typing tissues, filter paper and pads moon rock, press-pan, silk thread, decorative papers of various varieties, deluxe stationary such as deluxe stationary, writing pads, envelopes, card sheet, fancy and decorative.
X.	Starch,washing soda, lime.	Caustic soda, lime, rosin alum, glue sodium-silicate, optical bleaching agents, synthetic resins, starch, China clay, PVA, Titanium Dioxides, several other adhesives, dyes and pigments.

In comparison to other Village Industries the employment generation potential in Handmade Paper Industry is low. However if we compare between Handmade Paper and mill made paper, handmade paper certainly gives better employment avenue than the mill made paper. This is given in a comparative chart in the table given below:

	Handmade paper	*Mill made paper*
A. Investment on plant on per ton per annum production	12450	24850
B. Employment generation on invest of each Rs. One crore	980	130
C. Employment generation of each 1000 ton of produciton	1050	25
D. Import of machinery	nil	35%

Besides above, handmade paper replaces much lesser input than mill made paper and is eco-friendly. This is because of the fact that handmade paper does not eat away forest resources. The comparative statements are given below in the tabular form:

Resource input of production per ton

A. Forest based Raw materials like bamboo,wood etc. ton per annum production	Nil	2.5 to 3 ton
B. Coal	0.085 ton	1.50 ton
C. Electricity	150 kWh	2000 kWh
D. Water	38 cu. Mtrs	300 cu. Mtrs
E. Chemicals	0.0051 ton	0.8 ton

A. Environmental Impact		
Ecology	Nil	2.65 ton of dry forest based raw materials are used for manufacture of one ton of paper

B. Pollution		
Water Pollution	Insignificant	Highly polluted with toxicity
Air Pollution	Nil	Gaseous emission in all process of paper making.

However, if we do not restrict handmade paper production alone but we feel go further for value addition of the paper produced from the handmade paper, the employment generation the sky is the limit. Depending upon the type of production to be produced, paper showed not only that the earning will improve but also there will be improvement of employment generation. It also helps in better marketing of the handmade paper. In fact due to such product development the export of handmade paper in the country will increase upto a considerable extent, though the exact figure could not be ascertained since the figure is amalgamated with other facts. The estimated figures by value, items and destination are given below:

Export

The Industry has major say in Export also. The demand of Handmade paper, for its eco-friendly nature and global environmental awareness, is increasing day by day. KVIC is exporting Handmade paper directly and through its manufacturing units and even by merchant exporters. Handmade Paper is being exported in sheets as well as in converted forms. At present the export are being made to U.K., Germany, Italy, Holland, France, Sweden, U.S.A., Canada, Japan, Singapore, Hong Kong, Australia, New Zealand, Gulf countries etc. The Directorate of Handmade Paper Industry also undertakes export of handmade paper directly to various countries.

*HMP Exports from India—Trends**

1.	Upto 1991	Rs. 60 lacs
2.	1993-94	Rs. 5 crores
3.	1994-95	Rs. 8 crores
4.	Till 2000	Rs. 25 crores (Estimated)

A. Country-wise Exports

1.	U.S.A.	30%
2.	U.K.	15%
3.	Germay	20%
4.	Italy	5%
5.	Others	30%

Items of Exports

1. Drawing Paper
2. Mottled Paper
3. Carry bags
4. Fancy stationery with 100 per cent Non-wood and Recycled Papers.

This improvement of export has taken place due to in value addition of the paper but also gives special incentive provided by KVIC in addition to the incentives provided by export promotion council.

However we have to go long way to work on this sector. We have not done much for the quality assurance system in this sector. If the quality can be ensured it will not only increase the earnings but also ensure market demand. Quality does not mean bad quality alone. It may also mean that if we consume more material of thicker quality though the required earnings goes down. This also has to be worked out properly and proper input has to be given.

Handmade paper also consumes basically the cotton rags from the textile mills. In multi fibre design this is becoming increasingly difficult since the rags which is coming is increasingly mixed with synthetic fibre which does not give good quality. Good vegetable fibres are also available all over the country. If we work with these fibres further employment generation can be ensured. This aspect needs to be looked into. KVIC is constantly working on these aspects and new products are coming.

3

Development of Handmade Paper and the Machinery Thereof

G.K. GHOSH

Preamble

The paper used to be, and even now, the media of communication since the advent to civilization in this evolutional cycle. Stones and stone plates as well as wooden logs were the primitive materials used by the man to inscribe his feelings. Slowly and steadily man developed other base materials for writing such as palm leaves, cloth pieces or bricks, all for preserving his experiences, achievements and territorial indications. Further civilizations motivated the mankind to invent paper as we see now with much improvement.

The art of Handmade Paper making is an age-old craft, which had a minimal impact on the socio-economic structure of the society. The artisans who used to make paper were striving hard for the self-existence due to the onus the art carried along.

The name "PAPER" was evolved from the reed called "PAPYRUS" found on the banks of Nile river in Egypt. China enjoys the privilege of invention of Paper during 105 A.D. by T'sai Lun. Indians are credited to have used paper made from cellulose fibre in 3rd Century. It was during 7th Century that the knowledge spread to Japan but the rest of the World could know about paper only during the 8th Century. The craft gradually spread to other countries only after 8th Century.

In India paper making entered through two different routes from two origins.

The first route was through Eastern and North Eastern borders originating from China. As India exported the philosophy of Buddhism, due to this ancient paper making clusters came up around Tawang in Arunachal Pradesh, Bijonbari and Kalimpong. North of West Bengal which went further down to create cluster such as Bhagwan-gola in Murshidabad District, Dasghara in Hooghly District and Moinan in Howrah District of West Bengal. Most of these clusters faced natural death but Tawang, Kalimpong and Bijonbari are still surviving.

Other route was through North India with technology developed in Egypt which was introduced probably during 1420-1470. Paper making was first introduced in Kashmir from Samarkhund by King Zanul Abedin. The art of paper making mostly carried out by the Muslims called "Kagzis" who inhabited in hamlets known as Kagzipuras. Such hamlets were found in Kalpi, Sanganer, Junnar, Sawaimadhopur, Erandole during Mughal period when the art touched its zenith.

Subsequently the two influenced each other to create a new Indian concept of paper making.

The process adopted by the conventional Kagzis was crude and restricted to the home level only. The paper used to be produced from the available resources of raw materials like waste paper etc. The process and radical development in this sphere can be narrated as under:

Soaking

The Kagzis used to collect the waste paper and old waste cotton clothes. A lot of material was soaked in a soak pit for several days along with limestones to fibrillate the clothes and the paper.

Gradually due to the introduction of new technology the waste paper is slowly replaced by hosiery cuttings, cotton rags, agro waste materials as raw materials. Other cellulosic materials from agro wastes are also being used for making special types of papers. However, for using good raw materials to produce quality papers the raw materials like cotton rags need to be sorted out to small pieces, dusted, washed and cooked. For this purpose several standard machines like rag chopper, digesters, dusting machines and washing machines have been developed. The standardized machines now commonly used are given below.

Pulping

The substance thus obtained was transferred to a stone pit engraved in stone underground and stamped by feet using a lever called *dhenki.* This process was a crude method of pulping. The mashed material, *'the pulp'* was then transferred to baskets and cleaned. The cleaning was done on cloth piece tied on the waist of two persons standing in the opposite direction in the river. The pulp on the cloth piece is stirred rigorously to remove the dust, dirt or any other material in the pulp, which would mar the quality of the paper.

In the course of time more and more innovations in the field of machinery was witnessed and the traditional *dhenki* was replaced by the Hollander beater. The cylindrical roll of the beater having blades fixed vertically on the surface is fixed in a thorough of RCC construction with the help of parallel bars having worm wheels. The introduction of this machine has almost wiped out the drudgery and of course improved drastically the yield. The cleaning of the pulp is also done simultaneously with the help of a washing drum, which is affixed to the system with the help of a reducing gear.

The details of beater now being used by most of HMP units are given below:

Beater—30″ × 36″

Main parts—(1) Roller (with knives) 36″ dia, 30″ width, (2) Central shaft, (3) Cast iron pedestals with central lever to hold shaft, (4) Bed plate with knives, (5) Two U shaped girders for pedestal channel, (6) Washing drum 30″ width and 36″ dia with 40 mesh wire with angle iron stands, (7) Wooden hood to cover the roller, (8) Cement for beater to be constructed at site as per design, (9) Cast Iron V pulley for driving the beater.

Roller

30" width, 36" dia (whole roller machine cut with knives fitted). Weight of the roller—1.85 tonnes to 2 tonnes.

Blades—72 Nos. length 30"-3/8" thick M.S. Plate tempered to hardness 4" wide. Blades be fitted with interlocking system with wooden wedge fitted between two blades firmly on surface leaving the knives projected 2/8" above the surface of wedges. Side walls of the roller plate be covered with M.S. Plate of 3/8" thick by screws and 1" M.S. bar banger plates on both end surfaces. Central shaft M.S. Rod of 5" dia. All through the length 6'-4". Total length of shaft 8'. The shaft be tapered down to 4" dia. At both ends 10" from one end of shaft should have a perfect balancing. Rigid and sturdy (balancing weight be done by heavy cast iron discs 3 Nos. properly pinned and welded).

Pedestal

Rigid cast iron pulleys 4"×5"×2½" height. Without blow holes with a central lever of cast iron 4"×3½' long. Back end of which is fixed in a pin of 1½" dia. The front end is open fork like arrangement where the lifting screw is placed which is operated by worm gears at each end with a common shaft of 1" dia. M.S. rod to lift the roller up and down when in motion.

Bed Plate

Blades of above roller blade dimensions placed on a rigid wooden stand of 10" wide and 30" long 4½" height. The blades be fitted at 4 to 5 degrees angle to that of the roller blades (either V shaped or oblique position). The blades be machined as per the curve of the roller periphery. The whole set be encased in a M.S. box with a pair of iron wedges.

Washing Drum

30"× 36" diameter with wooden plank side walls. Inside 3 aluminium 14 gauge sheet scanning pans to pull the water out. The drum be covered first by 8 mesh supporting copper to brass wire and the top mesh of 35 mesh phosphor bronze or copper wire mesh with suitable arrangements of 1½" angle iron frame to lower it and lift up as per requirements.

Beater Trough

This part is constructed with brick and cement as per the drawing supplied by us at the spot where the machine is to be fitted. Construction of trough is of a highly skilled nature with the proper flow slopes, back fall slopes, and trap pitch. Bed plate fitting pouch and a door. The outlet pipes 2½ dia for pulp and for waste water. All such arrangements are shown in the drawing. Each manufacturer must have a drawing of each beater trough with him.

Hood

Semi circular wooden cover over the roller of the beater. It is made by ½" wooden strips of light wood joined each other for water proof and is covered on top with aluminium 14 gauge sheet or same with a wooden cover.

A 'Doctor' plate wooden tank is also fitted inside the hood at a proper angle and the place to help the flow of the pulp in the beater. Drawing is also supplied to make the hood. The distance of 4" be kept all round the roller while making the hood. Approximate weight of the whole machine including roller is 2600 kg. which produces 250 kg. of straws, bagasse etc. per charge in 2½ hours.

Baby beater with a table model 12"× 8" roller size with bed plate and parallel lifting arrangements trough made by M.S. plate 2/8" thick washing drum and hood. This is exact replica of a big beater, hence material should be taken in proportion of the roller size. This machine can be fitted on a table with a M.S. plate platform, run by a motor 1.5 HP to 2 HP weight of the machine 600 kg. This is useful in conducting experiments in making pulp from different raw materials.

Purpose

This is very important machine in the industry. Raw materials are beaten in the fine pulp. Simultaneously it can wash during beating time with washing drum. Any fibrous raw material can be beaten into pulp. Hence advantageous over the 'pulp' can make any type of paper or board as per the raw material taken for beating. The capacity of production of unit depends on the capacity of the beater. Motor—30 H.P. slip-ring type 960 RPM (Ideal peripheral speed of roll—3000 ft. per minute to decide its final RPM).

In case of waste paper pulping one more machine called hydrapulper was introduced for easy and fast pulping. The machine was a bigger replica of the modern day mixer and grinder. It had a vessel and in the bottom centre there was asset of rotating blades which used to crush and pulp the waste paper. The waste paper is fed in hydrapulper and foaming agent is added to remove ink particles if any through flotation system. The raw material is converted into pulp form in 1 to 2 hours period.

Lifting

The cleaned pulp then transferred to underground water tanks and stirred with a stick rigorously to avoid formation of knots in the pulp.

Modernisation made its impact on this process also which replaced the old time tanks with RCC tanks with agitators, which disallows the formation of knots in the pulp.

The uniform, consistent pulp is stored in the tanks and is ready for preparing the paper sheets. The process of lifting paper from the pulp was done on a grass mat known as **"Chhapri"**. These chhapris were made from a typical grass sticks woven together by nylon or cotton threads, locally by the kagzis.

Due to the advent of modern technology in the field of Handmade Paper slowly the Chhapris were replaced by Vats. The Vat is prevalent in the modern day Handmade Paper making also. The Vat is an equipment having a wooden or metal tank containing water. Wiremesh fixed on measured wooden frame called deckle. Same size upper deckle is fixed on the deckle containing wiremesh by the help of clamps to prevent the outflow of pulp. The entire system is suspended in the Vat though wire ropes connected to a lever operated by foot. Measured quantity of pulp is poured on the mould and stirred vigorously to prevent the formation of uneven surface layer of paper.

Details of Vats now being used by most of the units are given below:

Vats

Paper lifting device—wooden tank with ½" angle iron frame size of the tank 42"×56" (inside measure). False bottom resting frame inside the tank a fabrication of the angle iron 1½" and 3/8" iron strips tradle is to be made to fix up the 'Deckle' box of the mould. The side ends are suspended by 6 adjustable screws ¼" rod 6" long to a common 1" rod which lifts up and down with a common angle iron peddle.

Deckles and Mould

Deckle box is made to rest the mould inside. Bottom plank be ½" thick wooden plank. A complete bottom frame is made to fix this with ½" screw to the bottom frame. Similar 3 wooden frames are made to cover the mould on two sides with 'hinges'. One end is kept free to open the top frame to remove and insert the mould.

Mound

Paper lifting mesh—Teak wood frame of 1¼" broad and ½" thick wooden frame on back side of which the ribbed fabrication of small wooden stips are fitted. Out of this 8 mesh copper wire is stretched as supporting mesh. Last layer is covered with stretched copper or ph bronz wire 40 mesh with two small wooden handles at each side 2 Nos. per each Vat size 26"×34".

Purpose

Pulp is poured into the mesh when in water. Stir with hand then gradually the mould is lifted up with the help of the paddle. The water gets sucked in the tank and the pulp settles on the mesh. This is the 'wet pulp sheet'. Then the mould is taken out for couching on cloth. The operation is repeated.

Four sets of Vats are required. Weight of Vat (each) about 125 kg. Finish and rust proof coating be given. It should work smooth without any strain on a person.

Further development in this process as made by introduction of a semi-automatic machine called Cylinder Mould. The wet paper sheets are made on a machine called cylinder mould by passing the pulp on the running wire mesh. This is semi-mechanised process of handmade papermaking.

Couching

The sheet thus formed is transferred to cotton cloth one upon the other and similarly a pile of paper sheets is formed by sandwiching sheets in between two cloth pieces.

Out standard couching tables now in use are given below:

Couching Table

42"×36" wooden plank of ½" thick wood with angle iron frame 1½"×2½" height—4 Nos.

Purpose

To lay the wet sheet on the napkin or wooden felts such sheets are piled up before it is taken to hydraulic press.

Pressing

The sheets thus formed are piled one above the other with cotton napkins (felt) sandwiched in between. Heavy stone or weight is placed on the pile over a wooden plank so as to remove the excess water from the pile.

Development is done in this process by introduction of screw press which is replaced by power operated hydraulic press in the sheets. If the paper is made on cylinder mould this process can be avoided.

The details of standard hydraulic press and screw press commonly used now are given below:

Hydraulic Press

Parts—(1) Plate—M.S. 40"×50", (2) 2 Ram cylinders 9" dia, (3) welded frame work, (4) pumping unit, (5) oil tank, (6) Hydraulic fluid pining, pressure gauge, safety valve, operating valve, (7) Trolleys.

Plate—M.S. rigid plate 1" thick with welded fabrication ribs beneath to be suspended on the two rams with sockets.

Rams—9" dia with proper M.S. rigid casing machined properly to hold ram gliding inside with air tight fitness. Ram Travel—10" loading height 9" with cup washers underneath.

Frame work—Rigid M.S. girders above 9" width properly welded to make the side framework, make of R.S. loists channel with pumping unit.

Oil Tank—M.S. plate box type welded tank fitted inside the box in the pumping unit (with 4-6 plungers) fitted on to a crank shaft (Box 2½"×1"×1½") run by a driving V-belt pulley.

Pulley—2" face 2 V grooves, 1½" dia cast iron. Entire fabrication rigidly welded with strong supporting fabricating angle iron on top and bottom plates.

Trolleys

Angle iron legs ¾" height just ½" above the lowest resting point of the bottom plate. It should go easily on the bottom plate. The trolley is meant to load the wet posts of sheets to be pressed. 1" gap be left between the bottom plate and the framework to allow trolley to go in. The whole trolley is lifted with post of pressing. Total load on the 2 Rams—198-200 tonnes, P.S.I. of plungers 1500 kgs. to 2000 kg. maximum. Resultant pressure on the wet sheet required 120 kg. to 150 kg. per sq. inch. Total weight of the press—2600 kg. Machine be accurately fabricated. Care be taken to keep all parts in level. Plate, rams, top plate and frame must be in one level to avoid breakage or bending of any part during working.

Painting should be attractive and finish should be pleasing.

Purpose

This machine is used in removing water by pressing from the wet couched sheets of paper and board.

Motor—5 H.P. induction type.

Screw Press

Sample central screw movement press plate 36"×42" M.S. ½" plate rigidly strengthened by top girders welding or a good cast iron ribbed plate. Central Screw—4" dia. 2 T.P.I. acquire with cabstain thrust ibearing Side poles 4 Nos. 5" dia. M.S. rods. Top wheel 20". Operated by hand only. Good finish, trouble free working and good painting.

Purpose

To press wet sheets to remove water as well as to press glue sized papers. Total weight of the machine is 2000 kg.

Peeling and Drying

In olden days the semi-wet papers from the pile of paper is slowly separated and are then pasted on clean lime coated walls in shade with the help of a brush so as to dry them uniformly.

In the modern days the pile of pressed sheets are removed under the press and separated/peeled apart from the felt and loft dried for natural drying indoors.

Cleaning

The dried papers are sorted one by one to get rid of the damaged paper and dirt specks.

Surface Sizing

The paper in olden days was starch quoted with the help of a brush to prevent ink absorption.

Later on the starch was replaced by glue. But the process was bit different. The animal glue was made into a solution where the papers were dipped completely to prevent the ink clotting. This process is applicable only for high-grade papers like drawing papers, water mark certificate paper and for the papers which are to be preserved for long period.

However, in modern days the pulp itself is sized by using rosin in its soluble form (Rosin soap) as sizing agent and Alum as fixing agent in beater. By this way slowly the tub sizing or surfacing is reduced in the process drastically.

Paper produced on cylinder mould mainly using waste paper, as its raw material does not require this process hence can be skipped off.

Calendering

In the olden days the dry papers are collected and one by one they are polished by placing them on a curved wooden plank and rubbing by a smooth stone.

The dried paper is glazed passing through rotating chilled rolls by using zinc sheets in between the papers. However, few varieties of drawing paper does not required calendering.

Details of standard calendering machines now being used commonly are given below:

Calender Machine

Main parts—(1) Calender rolls (Bowls) 2 Nos., (2) Gear wheels—2 Nos. Pedestals, (3) Reduction gear wheel, (4) Driving V Pulley, (5) Counter weight lever system, (6) Platforms for paper post 2 Nos., (7) Side Pedestals—2 Nos.

Calendar Rolls

12" dia × 36" long rolls made of good cast iron without blow holes with Brinel's Hardness up to 200 with mirror polish on the surface (C.I. rolls are preferred).

Reduction Gear

Cast iron gear wheel with machines cut nitches. The teeth of the gear wheels be adjusted to the proper ratio to keep the final RPM of the rollers to 7 RPM. No faster speed is required.

Driving Pulley

Cast iron V Pulley dia and the grooves be adjusted to suit the resultant speed of the calendar rolls (*i.e.* 7 RPM).

Counter Weight Levers

M.S. plate fabrication to lift the rollers parallel when 'post' of sheets is inserted ¾" plate thickness with the fixing screws on each end of top calendar roll with cast iron pieces of weights for balancing.

Wooden Platform

½" thick wooden plank of 36"× 40" framed with rigid angle iron fitted with counter sinked screws. The top surface of plate be covered with thin 20 gauge zinc sheet or aluminium sheet. Adjustable bars be provided to change the angle or a platform to suit the intake of the 'post' of paper by ¼" square rods with 4 holes at the bottom to fit up the pins.

Side Pedestals

Rigid cast iron pedestals in two half on each side to accommodate rollers and base platform for foundation as per drawing.

Painting should be smooth and attractive. The finish of the machine be sophisticated. The roller when in motion should not give any 'noise' nor it should vibrate. It should work with perfect silence. Weight of the machine—2200 kg. Run with (10 HP motor at 960 RPM preferably) reversible switch arrangement.

Purpose of the Machine

This machine is used in making the sheet surface smooth and desired by the customer. The sheets are placed in between the zinc sheets and made in a 'post' of 30-40 sheets and this post is passed in between the rollers. It operates to and fro some time and imparts the glaze to the paper sheets.

Trimming and Packing

The edges of the paper is cut by a knife uniformly by a cutter before selling them. The cutting used to be done by affixing some limited number of papers between two wooden planks by nut bolts affixed on the planks outside the dimensions of paper so as to give the grip. The protruding edges of the papers are then cut by a sharp knife uniformly.

Standard cutting machines now being used commonly by various units are given below:

Paper Cutting Machine

42" cutting width, diagonal cutting with a set of 2 knives to be operated both by 2 HP motor or by hand. These cutting machines are made by many manufacturers and readily available in the market. It can be purchased and sent along with the other machines. Hence detailed specifications are not needed. They are sold as a complete set.

The above information is based on the technology in practice. In some areas even these machineries are not being used for various reasons. For example since machineries are power operated, it failed in Tawang in Arunachal Pradesh where power supply is doubtful. Before allotting these machineries it should have been assessed.

Even where these machineries are used it does not give desired result to the extent that there is limitations in product diversification due to mechanization.

There is need for continuous research to evolve proper machineries so that on one hand productivity should improve while on the other product diversification according to market demand is not hampered. There is also need for standardization of machineries so that maintenance becomes easy. For past few decades it is not being practiced. Such planning must be made involving manufacturers and all commercial units must keep a separate corpus fund from their profits for such R&D. Only then HMP shall progress and sustain itself to complete in global market.

4

Applications of Biotechnology in Pulp and Papermaking and Opportunities for the Handmade Paper Industry

R.K. JAIN, A.K. SHARMA and SUNITA CHAUHAN

Introduction

Biotechnology is a branch of science dealing with technical exploitation of living organisms and/or their products. It is the most relevant and promising science of today. Advantages of biotechnological processes over chemical processes are:

Biotechnological Processes	*Chemical Processes*
• Based on cleaner production techniques	• Highly polluting
• Minimum energy requirement	• Energy intensive
• Require less equipment	• Require multiplicity of equipment
• Compatible between stages and over all reduced cost	• Low compatibility between stages
• Are inherently more selective and specific having the key benefits of reduced side reactions, easy separation and negligible environmental effects.	• Are not so selective and have a wide range of side reactions and environmental effects.

Historical Perspective of Biotechnology in the Paper Industry

In the mid-70s, knowledge about the enzyme mechanisms involved in wood degradation was in its infancy. Suggestion to use enzymes in paper industry seemed out of reach. Economic feasibility of the production of enzymes was impossible. Since then, enormous progress has been made in Biosciences in general *i.e.* in Genetics, Molecular biology, Biochemistry and Microbiology. Production of enzymes is economically feasible. Enzymes from alkaliphillic and thermophillic microorganisms can now be cloned into efficient production systems. Micro-organisms can now be genetically changed to make them ideal for specific purposes. Enzymes can be designed to better catalyze industrially important reactions. Massive amount of efforts devoted over the past few decades to a better understanding of the enzymes produced by wood degrading micro-organisms for conversion and degradation of lignin, cellulose and hemicellulose have provided a fresh base for successful development of biotechnology in pulp and paper industry.

Due to the above advances, role of biotechnology in pulp and paper industry has increased tremendously over the last decade and several new biotechnology markets have been developed.Use of xylanase to aid in bleaching of chemical pulp was introduced by Viikari *et al.* in 1986.The technology is now in use at several mills worldwide. Use of xylanase can reduce chemical bleaching costs upto 20 per cent. For chlorine based technologies in kraft pulps, this may reduce AOX discharges by 5-20 per cent depending upon wood furnish and mill pulping conditions. Can increase final brightness of the pulp by 5-8 per cent over the control.

Present Status of Biotechnological Applications

S.No.	Process	Status
1.	Biological depithing of raw material	Commercial
2.	Biological pitch removal from wood chips	Commercial
3.	Enzymatic pitch removal from pulp	Commercial
4.	Xylanases for pulp bleaching	Commercial
5.	Improvement of pulp drainage by enzymes	Commercial
6.	Enzymatic deinking	Commercial
7.	Production of dissolving pulp using xylanase enzymes	Commercial
8.	Biofiltration for control of odorous emissions	Commercial
9.	Improving beatability of pulp with enzymes	Commercial
10.	Pulp bleaching with lignin oxidizing enzymes	Pilot scale
11.	Biopulping-mechanical/chemical	Pilot scale
12.	De-chlorination and de-toxification of bleach effluents	Pilot scale
13.	Tree improvement	Pilot scale
14.	Enzymatic debarking	Lab. scale
15.	Enzymatic retting of flax fibers	Lab. scale

Applications of Biotechnology

There are two ways in which Biotechnology can be helpful: (1) Direct approach, and (2) Indirect approach.

Direct Approach

It can aid in the betterment of various processes of papermaking. Some of the important applications are: biopulping, biobleaching, deinking, decolourization of effluents, improving the drainage of secondary fibres, biomethanation of spent liquors, debarking etc.

Biopulping

The process of biopulping includes the treatment of fibrous raw materials with ligninolytic organisms prior to conventional pulping processes. Advantages of biopulping are: improved strength properties, higher yield, reduced cooking chemicals and reduced refining energy. Organisms used include the strains of white rot fungi like *Cereporiopsis subvermispora, P.chrysosporium, P. ostreatus, Panus conchatus.C.subvermispora* is found to be the best suited organism for the purpose and has been used in large scale outdoor delignification of 50 metric ton chip pile at Forest Product Laboratory, U.S.A. The important features of the study were: 30 per cent energy saving, quality of paper from pretreated chips was better than that from the non-pretreated chips.

Biobleaching

Biobleaching involves the treatment of pulp with hemicellulases (most commonly xylanases) before the conventional bleaching sequences. Xylanases increase the accessibility of bleach chemicals to lignin removal. Advantages are: increased brightness ceiling, comparative/improved strength properties, decreased bleach chemical requirements, decreased toxicity of bleach effluents and decreased pollution load in the effluents. The enzymes having potential of biobleaching are ligninolytic enzymes (Lignin peroxidases, Manganese peroxidases, laccases) and Hemicellulases (Endo-1, 4-β-D-xylanase; 1,4-β-D-mannosidase; 1,4-α-D-glucosidase, β-D-glucuronidase; 2-D-galactosidase; Acetyl xylan esterase, Acetyl galacto gluco mannanesterase). Out of these, hemicellulases particularly the xylanases have been proved to be most suitable for the process and are being utilized commercially as well.

The first mill trial of India on xylanase prebleaching was conducted in a pulp and paper mill of Ballarpur Industries Ltd. (BILT) in 1992 using acidic xylanase enzyme produced by M/s. Biocon India Pvt. Ltd. Subsequently, several other mill trials were organized in different mills using different types of raw materials and practicing different pulping and bleaching processes using xylanase enzymes of different qualities including alkaline and thermotolerant enzymes. Some of those mills are: Century Pulp and Paper, Grasim mills, Central Pulp and Paper mills, Shreyans Paper mills and Varindra Agropaper mills.

Enzymatic Deinking

For recycling mills, conventional deinking methods have become inadequate because of the polymers used in laser and xerographic printing. There is an increasing dependence upon mechanical devices for breaking down the large, non-impact ink particles to be able to remove them by flotation or washing. These intensive mechanical forces are **energy demanding** and shorten the fibers **decreasing freeness and strength** of the paper formed from these fibers. Mixture of enzymes mostly cellulases have been implemented to substitute for chemical deinking of such furnishes and other furnishes such as old newsprint **(ONP)** and old magazine (**OMP)** are also successfully deinked using mixture of enzymes. **Enzynk process,** developed at University of Georgia (1998), has been found to be suitable for deinking all kinds of recycled paper. The company **Enzymatic Deinking Technologies (EDT)** has commercialized the enzymatic deinking technology in pulp and paper mills in United States, Europe and Asia and the market for this technique seems to be growing. The enzymes like lipases, esterases degrade vegetable oil based inks, pectinase, hemicellulase, cellulases are other such enzymes.

Improving the Drainage of Secondary Fibers

Drainage can be improved by controlled changes in cellulose, brought about by careful use of the enzymes (mixture of cellulase and xylansae). Cellulase and hemicellulase enzymes also reduce energy requirement during refining of chemical and mechanical pulps. Several commercial enzymes are available for the purpose. Today, the process is not economically viable. However, with rising power cost and a possible reduction in enzyme cost in the near future, the process seems to have great potential.

Decolourization of the Effluents

Not a single process is sufficient to completely decolourize coloured effluents. A proper combination of physical, chemical and biological methods is required. Among the biological processes, process termed as **MYCOR process** (Mycelial Colour Removal Process) is found to be very useful in this concern.

Debarking

Pectinases and hemicellulase enzymes are found to reduce energy requirements as much as 80 per cent during debarking. Poor infiltration of enzymes in the cambium of whole logs is a major difficulty. Pectinase and xylanase have been also used in processing plant fiber sources such as flax and hemp. At present, the fiber liberation is affected by retting. Replacement of slow natural retting by treatment with artificial mixture of enzymes could become a new fiber liberation technology.

Biogas from the Waste

Waste from the paper industry contains cellulosic materials so it can be utilized for generating fuel. The process is called as *Biomethanation.*

Indirect Approach

Biotechnology can indirectly help the pulp and paper industry through the production of improved fibrous raw materials with desired qualities using the techniques of Genetic Engineering and Tissue Culture.

Successful Commercialization of Biotech Process

It often takes time to convert a biotechnological breakthrough into a commercial venture. This is because a large number of technical and also important commercial and legislative criteria are to be satisfied in order to achieve commercial success. These include development of efficient process technology package through scale-up studies, starting from shake flask level along with inputs from molecular biology, optimization of unit operation, protection of the technology package and issues related to practicing the process on commercial scale when recombinant organisms are used.

Bipulping Consortium

Bipulping consortium formed in April 1987 to evaluate the commercial and economic feasibility of biomechanical pulping. The technological constraints in the way of commercialization of the huge pile of raw material, inoculation of the pile with sufficient amount of suitable fungus, maintenance of proper incubation conditions (temperature, *p*H, aeration, humidity etc.) throughout the pile for a long period of about two weeks. All these problems were mainly due to the high scale and continuous mode of operation prevailing in the mill sector. Even then, the consortium has come with the excellent solutions to solve all these problems.

Biobleaching

Biobleaching is comparatively easy to commercialize. However, the minor but important problems are:

- To use cellulase—less mutants (enzyme xylanase should be free of Cellulase).
- Proper mixing of enzyme solution with the pulp.
- Maintenance of proper *p*H and temperature for the required retention period of about one to two hours.
- Sufficient amount of enzyme. The enzyme is to be imported in India so it is costly and less economical until and unless the enzymes are indigenously produced.

Advantages of Biotechnology for HMP Industry

Fortunately what are the difficulties for the mill-sector, are the plus points for a handmade paper unit. Since it operates on small-scale and utilizes batch processes, neither, there would be any problem of scale-up nor of making the process continuous. The most important point is just to evaluate the potential in the specific context of handmade papermaking.

The biopulping economics estimated (through two 50-tonnes each, outdoor chip-pile trials) by the scientists of the consortium reveals an operating cost of 9.44US \$/ton of OD pulp besides the capital cost of 5.7×10^6 US\$ (for 600 TPD pulp) for the biopulping. As far as handmade paper industry is concerned, this cost would definitely be much lesser because firstly the maximum capacity of a HMP unit is 0.5 TPD so the capital cost would be reduced and secondly, the operating cost shall also be reduced drastically because neither there will be the need of ventilation blowers (as a small pile of raw materials could be mixed manually) nor the specific equipment (consisting of screw conveyors) would be required as suggested for the mill-sector. The whole operation appears to be rather simpler for a HMP unit. However, this all requires the proper basic studies to be done for its implementation.

Consideration that "sophisticated science of biotechnology is difficult to be accepted by the general mass of the handmade papermakers" is not true because they had been using it unknowingly in one or the other way from the very beginning.

- The Arabs used to disintegrate linen rags by placing them in heaps saturated with water and allowing a fermentation to take place.
- The Asiatic papermakers covered their papers with a thin coating of rice or wheat paste for sizing.
- For using bamboo, the Chinese used to strip off the leaves and shoots of canes, tied them into bundles and steeped in a pond until the green outer skin or bark could be removed. After splitting, the bamboo placed in layers with alternating layers of lime in a sunken pit (filled with water), were allowed to soak thoroughly for several months. Then after washing and beating, paper was made out of them.

- Even today, the extraction of jute fiber from green jute plants (*i.e.* retting) is done by steeping the plants in water for the sufficient time.

Thus, it was the unrefined form of biotechnology, where the handmade papermakers were somehow exploiting the action of existing microbes by manipulating the conditions of their processes. This all, implies that the potential of biotechnology has greater horizons and more hopes for the handmade paper industry.

Potential Applications of Biotechnology for Handmade Paper Industry

Having realized the great potential of Biotechnology in handmade paper sector, KNHPI has come forward to start work on biotechnology. The institute has established a Biotechnology laboratory of its own and is working in various areas of biotechnology in the specific context of handmade paper industry. The thrust areas chosen to work on presently are the following four important applications that have great potential for the handmade paper industry:

1. Biobleaching,
2. Biopulping/Biorefining,
3. Enzymatic Retting/Bioretting, and
4. Bioprocessing of shredded currency waste.

1. Biobleaching

Use of hemicellulases (mainly xylanases) as an aid in pulp bleaching (enzymatic prebleaching) is the biggest success story in the use of enzymes in the pulp and paper industry. Viikari *et al.* (1983) discovered that treating kraft pulps with fungal xylanases decreases the amount of bleach chemical required to attain a given brightness. Mill trials followed, confirming the laboratory results, and since the early 1990s xylanases have been used commercially in Scandinavia, Canada and Chile. The institutions like Central Pulp and Paper Research Institute (CPPRI), Saharanpur and Thapar Centre for Industrial Research and Development (TCIRD), Patiala have been putting sincere efforts for its commercialization in India also. Recently Dr. R.K. Jain and his team from CPPRI have conducted successful mill-scale trials of enzymatic prebleaching in few of the Indian paper mills.

The effect of hemicellulases in bleaching is based on the modification of pulp hemicelluloses, enhancing the removal of lignin in chemical bleaching. It has been proposed that the action of xylanases is due to the partial hydrolysis of reprecipitated xylan or to removal of xylan from the lignin-carbohydrate (LC) complexex. However, these hypotheses are not mutually exclusive *i.e.* relocated xylans may contain LC complexes and both mechanisms would allow the enhanced diffusion of entrapped lignin from the fiber wall. In addition, it has been suggested that the hemicellulase treatment removes chromophoric groups from the pulp.

Looking into the great potential in the technology of enzymatic prebleaching, KNHPI also started studies in this area with special emphasis on the raw materials and pulping procedures being utilized in the handmade paper industry. The institute has conducted extensive studies in the area of biobleaching using the enzymes produced at the institute's laboratory as well as those samples available commercially in the market. Pulps produced from a variety of raw materials like wheat straw, rice straw, jute, banana, paper mulberry, bagasse, bhimal etc. have been studied to see their biobleaching response with different enzyme samples. Almost all the pulps studied have shown gain in brightness points as compared to the respective controls without any adverse effect on their strength properties. Overall it has been found that the process of enzymatic prebleaching could result into:

- A gain of 3-4 points in the brightness of the enzymatically treated pulp as compared to the control pulp.

- A possibility of saving up to 25 per cent of the bleaching chemical (Hydrogen peroxide) to achieve a brightness value in the enzyme-treated pulp equivalent to that of the control pulp.
- Strength properties of the treated pulps were found to be slightly better as against those of the control pulp samples.
- The bleach effluents were also found to better in terms of the pollution parameters like BOD and COD.
- On calculating the economics in the case of enzymatic prebleaching of banana pulp, it was found that the enzymatic route required only one rupee per kg. of pulp as the extra investment. Out of this one rupee investment, enzyme cost is only 20 paise per kg. of pulp, rest is the cost of heating energy and the cost of adding acid to maintain *p*H.

Though this one rupee investment is nothing when we see the benefits of the enzyme usage for bleaching still the studies are being carried out at the institute to reduce this cost further by way of putting efforts to eliminate the use of acid and heating during enzymatic prebleaching of the handmade paper pulps. Efforts are being made to evaluate the xylanases that could work at ambient *p*H and temperature.

Table 4.1: Brightness Gain Observed in the Treated Pulp of Banana

Parameters	*Control*	*Treated*
Bleaching dose, % H_2O_2 on OD pulp	2.0	2.0
Brightness, % ISO	53.02	55.88
Gain in brightness, Points	—	2.86

Table 4.2: Savings in Bleach Chemical in Treated Banana Pulp

Parameters	*Control*	*Treated*
Bleaching dose, % H_2O_2 on OD pulp	2.0	1.5
% H_2O_2 consumed	71.85	74.98
Brightness, % ISO	52.82	53.62
% Saving in chemical	—	**25%**

Table 4.3: Physical Strength Properties of the Treated and Control Banana Pulp

Parameters	*Control (2% H_2O_2)*	*Treated (2% H_2O_2)*	*Treated (1.5% H_2O_2)*
Tensile index (Nm/gm)	63.16	75.96	67.75
Tear index (mN.m²/gm)	10.55	16.40	12.33
Burst index (kPa.m²/gm)	4.06	5.66	4.17
Double fold	16,148	23,740	16,105

2. *Biopulping/Biorefining*

The process of biopulping involves microbial treatment (specifically white rot fungi) of the fibrous raw material before the conventional pulping process. Due to their ligninolytic nature, white rot fungi metabolizes lignin from the raw material to a little or great extent depending upon the efficacy of the fungal treatment during the incubation period. As a result, there occurs a reduction in the requirement of pulping chemical during pulping and also in the cooking time required. Besides, a saving in the beating energy also results with an improvement in the strength properties. With the present stress on the use of alternative raw materials for making handmade paper and biobleaching in their processing, KNHPI is planning to work on the biopulping aspects in the near future. However, with an aim to develop a suitable technology or process for immediate implementation in the industry, KNHPI started some studies in the area of biorefining in the recent past.

It has been reported that the biorefining or enzymatic refining of virgin or recycled fibers can increase the paper strength, expand the surface area, improve the inter-fibre bonding, develop the freeness level and decrease the fibre fines. It has also been observed that pulp treatment with cellulase causes pulp fiber shortening and results into lower refining energy requirements to achieve a given drainage target. These advantages are reported to achieve with no adverse effect on physical properties of the cellulase-treated pulps.

Keeping in view of the extensive energy consumption during beating of the hosiery waste or cotton rags, traditionally used raw material for making handmade paper, the institute has evaluated certain identified enzymes for treating the hosiery waste. The institute has conducted both the laboratory and pilot plant trial besides a field trial of evaluating the effect of enzyme treatment on different samples of white and coloured hosiery waste besides the denim waste. This kind of enzymatic treatment has shown great promise in saving the energy while beating because the enzyme treatment could result into a saving of about 16-21 per cent of the beating energy as compared to the control. Overall advantages found to be were as below:

- A significant amount of saving in the beating energy.
- Better fibrillation.
- Improvement in strength properties.
- Improvement in pulp-drainability.

Table 4.4: Energy Consumption and Savings in Energy with White Hosiery Pulp

Parameters	*Control*	*Treated*
Consistency	2%	2%
Time taken to beat to CSF-350 ml.	3 hours	2.20 hours
Energy Consumption, kWh/ton of pulp	2240	1640
Savings in Beating Energy	Nil	26.8%

Table 4.5: Physical Strength Properties of the Control and Treated Pulp

Parameters	*Control*	*Treated*
Tensile index	21	20
Burst index	2.4	2.3
Tear index	21	26
Brightness, % ISO	96	96

3. *Enzymatic Retting*

With the growing demand of handmade papers made out of natural fibers, there is an urgent need of a sustainable supply of good quality natural fibres. Presently, the fibre being used for making handmade paper is extracted either mechanically or by submerging the plant parts under water or soil for over a long period of about 15-30 days, thereby creating the problem of water pollution.

Bio-retting process, which involves the use of certain enzymes for treating raw materials; holds greater promise for extraction of fibre. The quality of handmade paper produced from the fibre extracted from the lignocellulosic raw materials is found to be superior in terms of physico-chemical and strength properties, which could find applications in value added products. Encouraged with the preliminary studies carried out at KNHPI on bio-retting of Ankara plant, the institute has now extended its studies on various other fibres like banana, paper mulberry and whole bhimal, used for handmade papermaking, with an ultimate aim to demonstrate the process at Pilot plant/ industrial level. The potential benefits of bioretting were found to be as given below:

- Higher yield of fiber through enzymatic route.
- Better quality of fiber obtained.
- Reduction in the problem of water pollution.
- Possibility to use the same enzyme/retting liquor twice or thrice for extracting the fibre from fresh lots of plant parts used.

The process of enzymatic retting or bio-retting has been found to be equally effective in a range of raw materials tested like paper mulberry, Bhimal, Calotropis, Daphne etc. Besides, this kind of enzyme treatment was found to be effective in improving the quality of the rough banana fibre also as could be observed by better strength properties and higher brightness obtained when the banana fibre was treated with these enzymes prior to pulping.

Table 4.6: Comparison of Fiber Yield of Bhimal

Parameters	*Whole Bhimal (Conventional process)*	*Whole Bhimal (Bio-retted)*	*Bhimal Bark (From conventional retting process)*	*Bhimal Bark (Bio-retting process)*
Fiber yield,%	20	30	40	53

Table 4.7: Comparison of Fiber Yield of Bhimal with Commercial and Indigenous Enzyme

Parameters	*Commercial Enzyme*	*Indigenous Enzyme*
Fiber Yield,%	18% of Wood 56% of Bark	29% of Wood 60% of Bark

4. *Bioprocessing of Shredded Currency Waste*

The institute has already developed and patented a simple technology for recycling shredded currency waste of Reserve Bank of India (RBI).This process involves pressurized digestion and beating or refining of the pulp obtained. With a view to eliminate the use of chemicals and steam, certain identified enzymes have been evaluated on the shredded currency waste. The results have been very encouraging as the pulp obtained after enzyme treatment under optimized conditions has been found to be having better brightness and strength properties as compared to that obtained by pressurized digestion. The benefits observed with the application of enzymes while processing shredded currency waste were as below:

- A complete elimination of the stage of pressurized digestion, being used in the conventional process.
- Elimination of the use of chemicals like Sodium hydroxide, Hydrogen peroxide and Sodium Silicate, being used in the conventional process.
- Better sheet-formation with slightly improved strength properties.
- The process thus helps in reducing the pollution load and results into a better process in terms of eco-friendliness, while improving the drainage of the pulp obtained.

Table 4.8: Comparison of Strength Properties of Conventionally Cooked and Enzymatically Processed Shredded Currency Pulp

Parameters	*A Conventionally Cooked*	*B Enzymatically Pulped*
Tensile index	14.65	21.67
Tear index	7.05	6.99
Burst index	0.99	1.11
Double fold	27	40

Conclusion

Biotechnology is going to prove a boon for handmade paper industry. On one hand, where paper mills in India may take time to switch over to biotechnological applications, it can be immediately introduced in handmade paper industry. Need is to have a detailed study oriented specifically to the handmade paper industry *i.e.* using the prevailing raw materials and pulping procedures of the industry.

5

Energy Conservation in Handmade Paper during Beating Process
A Preliminary Study

BALESHWER PRASAD and M.E. KHAN

Introduction

At present about 95 per cent of the handmade paper in the country is being produced from cotton hosiery waste. The cost of the production of the paper from this raw material depends upon the factors such as cost of raw material, labour, electricity etc. Power consumption contributes to about 25-30 per cent of the total cost of production. In almost all the units, beating of the fibres is done in Hollander type of beaters. The power consumption being of the order of 1-1.5 kWh/kg. This power consumption during beating is extremely high and as much as the power being consumed in a big paper mill. It was in this context studies were initiated on optimization of process parameters to reduce the energy consumption during the fibre beating. The studies apart from reducing the cost of paper will also result in energy saving thereby reducing the impact on environment. Results of preliminary studies are being reported.

Beating of Pulp

Pulps beating is a mechanical treatment of pulp fibres to develop the optimum papermaking properties, which in turn depend upon the product being produced.

Beating of fibre is very important before making paper. This operation increases the strength of the fibre to fibre bonding by increasing the surface area of the fibres. Most strength properties increase with beating, however, tearing strength which is highly dependent on the strength of the individual fibres decreases with beating.

Beating process is dependent upon the:

- Consistency of the stock.
- *p*H and Temperature of the stock.
- Type and composition of the fibre.
- Type and design of the equipment.

Handmade paper industry mostly uses Hollander types of beaters for processing the hosiery fibres. Preliminary survey conducted revealed that proper attention is not being given to important variable like consistency during beating of fibres. Since stock consistency is very important in terms of paper quility and energy input, it was decided to initially conduct the optimization studies on this aspect.

Experiments

In first set of experiments hosiery waste samples were taken in a small beater of capacity 6 kg. pulp, at three different consistencies of 2.5, 3.0 and 3.5 per cent. Standard hand sheets prepared and evaluated for strength characterisitcs following the standard procedure. The results are recorded in Table 5.1.

Data on industrial beating of the hosiery waste was collected from three different handmade units. The results are recorded in Table 5.2. Strength properties of the pulp evaluated under standard conditions is recorded in Table 5.3. This was followed by conduting beating trials at a higher pulp consistency of 3.0 per cent in one of the industrial units. Pulp evaluation data is recorded in Table 5.5.

Results and Discussions

A perusal of Table 5.1, which gives the laboratory results of beating the pulps, reveals that time of pulp beating to 300 ml CSF at 2.5, 3.00 and 3.5 per cent consistencies were 3.5, 4.0 and 3.75 hrs respectively. Since there is no provision for measuring the power consumption in the small beater, time of beating of pulp to 300 ml CSF has been taken as a measure of energy consumption. With respect to strength characteristices, best results were obtained by beating the pulp at 3.5 per cent consistency with respect time of beating to 300 ml. CSF and strength characteristics of pulp. This is a normal phenomena as, higher consistency beating produces better fibrillation, less fibre cutting, resulting in better fibre to fibre bonding reflected in higher strength properties. From these results, it is clear that under the conditions studied optimum results with respect to strength and energy were obtained by beating the fibre at 3.5 per cent consistency.

Table 5.1: Beating Consistency Optimization

Consistency (%)	*Beating time (hrs)*	*CSF (ml)*	*Tensile Index (Nm/gm)*	*Tear Index (mN.m²/gm)*	*Burst Index (kPa. m²/gm)*	*Double Fold (No.)*	*Brightness (%)*	*Basis Weight (gm/m²)*
2.5	3.50	330	23.6	12.08	1.66	126	84.0	64
3.0	4.00	320	25.04	13.13	1.69	168	84.5	70.8
3.5	3.75	300	28.48	12.83	2.05	584	83.0	70

Table 5.2 presents a comparative data of beating of hosiery waste being followed in three different units of the industry. All these units are processing the fibre in exactly identical machines and are producing more or less similar products.

Beating process in the handmade paper industry is monitored by the time of beating at a pulp consistency of a round 2.6 per cent. As could be seen beating time is 4.5 hrs. and 5.0 hrs. and pulp consistency in all cases being around 2.6 per cent resulting in pulp freeness of around 600 ml CSF. Generally, as a standard practice the beating process is

Table 5.2: Industrial Pulp Beating Data

S. No.	*Unit*	*I*	*II*	*III*
1.	Date of visit and sample collected	01-06-2004	02-08-2004	16-02-2005
2.	Name of raw materials	White cotton hosiery waste	White cotton hosiery waste	White cotton hosiery waste
3.	Size of Hollander Beater	30"×36"	30"×36"	30"×36"
4.	Electric Motor installed	30 H.P.	30 H.P.	30 H.P.
5.	Quantity raw material/ charge	100 kg.	80 kg.	100 kg.
6.	Type of Paper of manufactured	150 GSM	250 GSM	250 GSM
7.	Beating Time	4.5 hrs.	4.5 hrs.	5.0 hrs.
8.	Consistency of Pulp	2.60%	2.70%	2.65%
9.	Final Freeness of Pulp	625 ml	650 ml	610 ml
10.	Total energy consumption	100 kWh	100 kWh	112 kWh
11.	Energy consumption/kg. of pulp	1.00 kWh	1.25 kWh	1.12 kWh
12.	Cost of energy/kg of pulp	Rs. 5.00	Rs. 6.25	Rs. 5.60

monitored by degree CSF of pulp. However in the handmade paper industry this is not being followed. As indicated by the results recorded in Table 5.3, since the higher degree of beating *i.e.* around 600 ml. CSF was maintained in the industry. They are not able to attain optimum results with respect to strength characteristics, which are generally obtained at lower freeness levels of around 350 ml. CSF Based on the above results, further studies were taken up in the industrial unit-1. As a first step, the pulp consistency in the beater was kept at 3 per cent. At this higher consistency, 120 kg. of pulp could be charged in the beater as compared to 100 kg. at 2.6 per cent consistency. The fibre was beaten for the same period of time *i.e.* 4.5 hrs. The resulting freeness was 400 ml CSF. Results recordes in Table 5.4 show that by increasing the consistency from 2.6 per cent to 3.0 per cent, there is almost 20 per cent saving in energy consumption during beating and also resulting in improved pulp quality as reflected by the strength properties recorded in Table 5.5.

Table 5.3: Strength Characteristics of the Industrial Pulp

S. No.	Unit	I	II	III
1.	Consistency%	2.60	2.70	2.65
2.	Beating time hrs.	4.5	4.5	5.0
3.	Freeness (C.S.F.) ml.	625	650	610
4.	Tensile Index (Nm/gm)	14.18	12.95	13.64
5.	Tear Index (mN.m²/gm)	12.15	13.13	10.58
6.	Burst Index (kPa.m²/gm)	0.21	0.27	0.25
7.	Double Fold Nos.	22	62	34
8.	Brightness% ISO	87.0	86.5	88.6

Table 5.4: Study on Beating of Pulp at Higher Consistency of 3%

S. No.	Unit-I	Consistency of Pulp at 2.60%	Consistency of Pulp at 3.5%
1.	Date of visit and sample collected	01-06-2004	17-02-2005
2.	Name of raw materials	White cotton hosiery waste	White cotton hosiery waste
3.	Size of Hollander Beater	30"×36"	30"×36"
4.	Elctric Motor installed	30 H.P.	30 H.P.
5.	Quantity raw material	100 kg. per charge of beater	120 kg. per charge of beater
6.	Type of page of manufactured	150 G.S.M.	150 G.S.M.
7.	Beating Time	4.5 hrs.	4.5 hrs.
8.	Final Freeness of Pulp	625 ml	400 ml.
9.	Total energy consumption	100 kWh	100 kWh
10.	Energy consumption/ kg. of pulp	1.00 kW	0.83 kW
11.	Cost of energy/kg. of pulp	Rs. 5.00	Rs. 4.16

Table 5.5: Comparative Pulp Strength Properties at Different Beating Consistency

Consistency (%)	Beating time (hrs)	CSF (ml)	Tensile Index (Nm/gm)	Tear Index (mN.m²/gm)	Burst Index (kPa. m²/gm)	Double Fold (No.)	Brightness (%)
2.60	4.50	625 ml	14.18	12.15	0.21	62	87.0
3.00	4.50	400 ml	26.43	20.26	1.44	165	87.5

Further it was also observed in some cases that the industry is not able to utilized full capacity of the equipment resulting in higher energy consumption and reduced production. This is clear from Table 5.2, where unit-II is able to process only 80 kg. of fibre per charge, as compared to other units who are processing 100 kg. pulp per charge each, in equipments having exactly same dimensions. This was observed to be due to improper design of the beater trough. There is therefore requirement for modification and standardization of equipment design.

Observations

From the above preliminary studies it is observed that beating consistency of around 2.6 per cent is being maintained for rag fibres, which is on the lower side. To attain optimum energy consumption as well as optimum pulp quality, beating consistency of over 3.00 per cent is recommended for better results. Beating process needs to be properly monitored to get a uniform pulp quality and also lower energy consumption. This monitoring is presently being done by the time of beating whereas monitoring should be by measuring the greeness at regular intervals by means of a Canadian Standard Freeness (CSF) Tester which is a simple mechanical instrument, easy to operate and is readily available in the country at a nominal price of Rs. 30,000 to 35,000 approximately.

To maintain the product uniformity and productivity, design modification and standardization of beaters for handmade paper is essential.

6

Machinery and Equipment for Handmade Paper Making

BALESHWER PRASAD

Introduction

Machinery and equipment is an important part of any industry from the progress point of view. One of the main steps is to select the right machinery and equipment keeping in view the size, capacity and cost of the equipment. This paper deals with the details, capacity, horsepower required and approximate cost and these are the basic requirements of an entrepreneur for establishing a unit or installing new equipment. These would be beneficial in proper capacity utilization of the machinery and equipment which effect the economy. This would also result in safer operations and production by reducing/eliminating system interruptions and equipment breakdowns.

List of Machinery and Equipment

- Rag Chopper
- Digester
- Hollander Beater
- Paper Making Auto Vat
- Press Machine
- Paper Dryer (Tausoki)
- Calender Machine
- Paper Cutting Machine

Process Flow Diagram

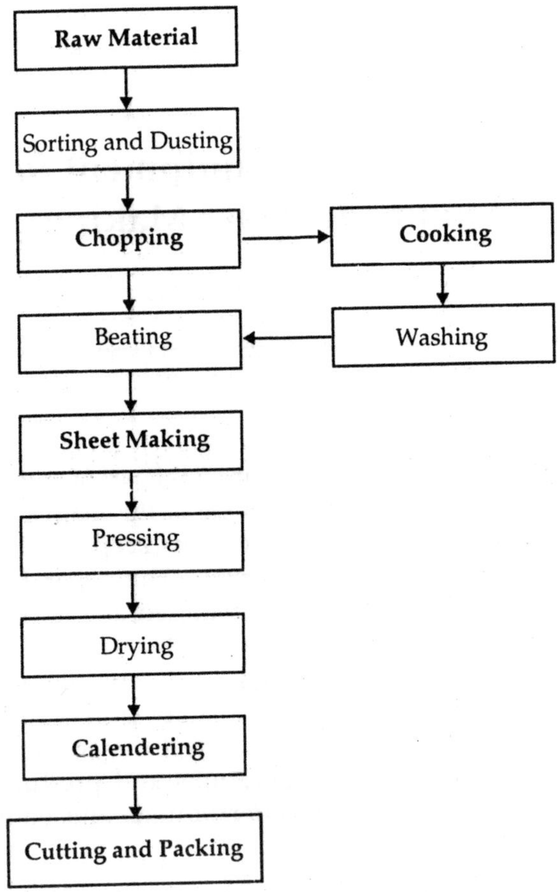

DETAIL SPECIFICATIONS

RAG CHOPPER

S. No.	*Size of Chopper*	*Details*	*Capacity*	*Req. HP*	*Appx. Cost*
1.	Size of Knife 10"	**Revolving Knives**—4/6 Nos. of hard steel, 10" length and 3" width fitted on central heavy cast iron roll. Each knife is fitted to edge of each and countersunk at angle-4° to central shaft of 2" to 2.1/2" dia. **Stationary Knife**—fitted to the bedplate with a sliding screw arrangement. **Feed Roll**—10" wide and 3.1/2" dia. With spring attached to each side and adjustable screw run with help of ratchet wheel drive or chain drive. Complete feeding platform or feeding conveyer and discharge chute. **Iron Frame**—rigid M.S. angle iron frame suitable to withstand the load. **Ball Bearing**—two standard make ball bearings for shaft. **Cast Iron Pulleys**—2 Nos. 18" dia. and 2" face. One pulley having 'A' section two V-groves another one-counter weight flywheels. **RPM of Chopper**—150 to 200.	40-50 kg/hr	3 HP	30,000/- to 35,000
2.	Size of Knife 12"	**Revolving Knives**—4/6 Nos. of hard steel, 12" length and 4" width fitted on central heavy cast iron roll. Each knife is fitted to edge of each and countersunk at angle-4° to central shaft of 2.1/2 to 3"dia. **Stationary Knife**—fitted to the bedplate with a sliding screw arrangement.	80-90 kg/hr	5 HP	40,000 to 45,000

S. No.	*Size of Chopper*	*Details*	*Capacity*	*Req. HP*	*Appx. Cost*
		Feed Roll—12" wide and 3.1/2" dia. with spring attached to each side and adjustable screw run with help of ratchet wheel drive or chain drive. Complete feeding platform or feeding conveyer and discharge chute. **Iron Frame**—right M.S. angle iron frame suitable to withstand the load. **Ball Bearing**—two standard make ball bearings for shaft. **Cast Iron Pulleys**—2 Nos. 24" dia. and 3" face. One pulley 'A' section two V-groves another one-counter weight flywheels. **RPM of Chopper**—180 to 220.			
3.	Size of Knife 14"	**Revolving Knives**—6 Nos. of hard steel, 14 to 15" length and 4" width fitted on central heavy cast iron roll. Each knife is fitted to edge of each and counter-sunk at angle-4° to central shaft of 3.1/2 to 4"dia. **Stationary Knife**—fitted to the bedplate with a sliding screw arrangement. **Feed Roll**—14" wide and 4" dia. with spring attached to each side and adjustable screw run with help of ratchet wheel drive or chain drive. Complete feeding platform or feeding conveyer and discharge chute. **Iron Frame**—rigid M.S. angle iron frame suitable to withstand the load. **Ball Bearing**—two standard make ball bearing for shaft. **Cast Iron Pulleys**—2 Nos. 24" dia. and 4" face, one pulley 'C' section fourV-groves another one-counter weight flywheels. **RPM of Chopper**—220 to 240.	13-150 kg/hr	7.5 HP	50,000 to 60,000

HOLLANDER BEATER

S. No.	*Size of Beater*	*Details*	*Capacity*	*Req. HP*	*Appx. Cost Excluding Motor*
1.	16"×20"	**Type**—Portable, M.S/S.S fabricated trough **Roll Size**—16"face and 20" dia. **Fly Knives**—52 Nos. **Bed Plate Knives**—9 Nos. **Bed Box**—S.S. fabricated **Shaft**—EN-8 **Blade Thickness**—6 to 8 mm. **Size of Washing Drum**—dia. 15", face 11.5" **Top Mesh of Washing Drum**—S.S.-304 of 40 mesh **Rotor Stand**—M.S. fabricated with complete system for lowering and lifting arrangement. **RPM of Rotor**—240 to 250 **Rotor Pulley**—3V -grooves pulley **Rotor Hood**—M.S./S.S. fabricated **Bearings**—2 Nos., double ball bearing. **Trough**—Civil construction	8-10 kg/ charge	5 HP 960 rpm	70,000 to 75,000 (MS) 90,000 to 95,000 (S.S.)
2.	18"×24"	**Roll Size**—18" face and 24" dia. **Fly Knives**—56 to 60 Nos. **Bed Plate Knives**—7 Nos. **Bed Box**—M.S. fabricated. **Blade Thickness**—8 to 10 mm. thick. **Shaft**—EN-8, dia. 3" to 3.5", length 7 to 7.5 ft. **Size of Washing Drum**—dia. 24", face 16" **Top Mesh of Washing Drum**—304 of 40 mesh **Rotor Stand**—M.S. fabricated with complete system for lowering and lifting arrangement. **RPM of Rotor**—240 **Rotor Pulley**—3V groove pulley with dia. 20-24"	40 to 50 kg./ charge	10 HP 960 rpm	85,000 to 95,000

S. No.	*Size of Beater*	*Details*	*Capacity*	*Req. HP*	*Appx. Cost Excluding Motor*
		Rotor Hood—Wooden Fabricated **Rotor Bearings**—Double roller bearing 2 Nos. **Trough**—Civil construction			
3.	24"× 30"	**Roll Size**—24" face and 30"dia. **Fly Knives**—64 Nos. **Bed Plate Knives**—8 to 9 Nos. **Bed Box**—M.S. fabricated. **Blade Thickness**—8 to 10 mm. thick **Shaft**—EN-8,dia. 4.5 to 5", length 8.5 ft. **Size of Washing Drum**—dia. 36", face 28" **Top Mesh** S.S.-304 of 40 mesh **Rotor Stand**—Cast Iron complete system for lowering and lifting arrangement. **RPM of Rotor**—240 **Rotor Pulley**—4 V-grooves pulley with C section dia. 24" **Rotor Hood**—Wooden Fabricated **Bearings**—Double roller bearing 2 Nos. **Trough**—Civil construction	90-100 kg/ charge	5-20 HP 900 rpm slip-ring motor	1,20,000 to 1,25,000
4.	30" × 36"	**Roll Size**—30" face and 30", face 28" **Top Mesh**—S.S.-304 of 40 mesh **Rotor Stand**—Cast Iron complete system for lowering and lifting arrangement. **RPM of Motor**—185-190 **Rotor Pulley**—4 V-grooves pulley with C section dia. 30" **Rotor Hood**—Wooden Fabricated **Bearings**—Double roller bearing 2 Nos. **Trough**—Civil construction	140-150 kg/ charge	25-30 HP 960 rpm slip-ring motor	1,55,000 to 1,60,000

PRESS MACHINE

S. No.	*Type*	*Details*	*Capacity*	*Req. HP*	*Appx. Cost (Rs.)*
1.	Screw press (Manually operated press)	Simple central screw movement **Plate Size**—36"× 42"×1/2" thick (M.S) Rigidly strengthened by top girders welding or good cast iron ribbed plate **Central Screw**—4" dia.2 TPI square with capstan thrust bearing **Side Rods**—4" No. 4"dia M.S. rods **Top Wheel**—20" dia. operated by hand **Total Weight of Machine**—2000 kg.	50-100 sheets/ cycle	—	30,000 to 40,000
2.	Screw Press (Motorized)	Simple central screw movement press **Plate Size**—36"× 42"×1/2" thick (M.S.) Rigidly strengthened by top girders welding or good cast iron ribbed plate **Central Screw**—4" dia. 2 TPI square with capstan thrust bearing. **Side Rods**—4 No. 5" dia. M.S. rods **Drive**—Worm wheel 30 teeth × 3 D.P. with worm. **Motor Pulley**—30" dia. two grooves 'B' section **Main Pulley**—18" dia. two grooves 'B' section	100 to 150 Sheets/ cycle	3 HP 960 RPM	50,000 to 60,000
3.	Hydraulic press	**Plate Size**—40"×42"×1" thick (MS), Bottom -38"× 42"× 1" thick (MS), Plates reinforced with 12 mm ribs to withstand pressure.	Capacity 60 MT working pressure 40-50 MT	3HP 960 rpm	1,60,000 to 1,70,000

S. No.	*Type*	*Details*	*Capacity*	*Req. HP*	*Appx. Cost (Rs.)*
		Channels Size—8"×3"×4" (to support press) **Railings**—for trolly movement **Ram**—8.5" dia, length 18" (sealing washer) **Piston Displacement**—8" to 10" **Power Pack System**—of standard make with gear pump, NRV, release valve, strainer with pressure gauge, safety valve, controlled valve, Hydraulic pipe etc. complete in all respect.			
4.	Hydraulic press	**Plate Size**—Top -40"× 42" × 1" thick (MS), Bottom -40"×42"×1" thick (MS) Plates reinforced withstand pressure **Channels Size**—8" × 3" × 4" (to support press) **Railings**—for trolley movement **Ram**—10.5" dia, length 18" (sealing washer) **Piston Displacement**—8" to 10" **Power Pack System**—of standard make with gear pump, NRV, release valve, strainer with pressure gauge, safety value, controlled value, Hydraulic pipe etc. Complete in all respect.	Capacity 100 MT	5HP 960 rpm	1,80,000 to 1,90,000

CALENDER MACHINE

S. No.	*Size of Machine*	*Details*	*Capacity*	*Req. HP*	*Appx. Cost (Rs.)*
1.	Roll Size 9"dia.× 30" length	• Machine comprising of 2 solid C.I./ forged steel roll and polished with Brinel's hardness up to 200°	300 sheets/ hr	3/5 HP 960 rmp	1,00,000 to 1,10,000

S. No.	*Size of Machine*	*Details*	*Capacity*	*Req. HP*	*Appx. Cost (Rs.)*
		• Supported by gunmetal bushes housed in C.I./MS housing. • Pressure application by spring and counter weight laver system. • C.I. spur gear and drive pinion on one side and broad teeth gears on other side give uniform movement to top roller • Reduction grearbox of standard makes to reduce the speed of roll and work the machine with 10 to 15 rpm. • Weight of each rolls not less than 350 to 400 kg. • The total weight of the machine should be around 1400 to 1500 kg.			
2.	Roll 12" dia. × 36" length	• Machine comprising of 2 solid C.I./forged steel roll and polished with brinel's hardness up to 200° • Supported by gunmetal bushes housed in C.I./M.S. Housing. • Pressure application by spring and counter weight laver system. • C.I. spur gear and drive pinion on one side and broad teeth gears on other side to give uniform movement to top roller • Reduction gearbox of standard makes to reduce the speed of roll and work the machine with 12 to 15 rpm. • Weight of each rolls not less than 600 kg. • The total weight of the machine should be round 2000 kg.	400 sheets/ hr	5/7.5 HP 960 rpm	1,60,000 to 1,70,000

DIGESTER

S. No.	*Size of Machine*	*Details*	*Capacity*	*Req. HP*	*Appx. Cost (Rs.)*
1.	Stationary	**Type**—Vertical, stationary, vomiting with false bottom perforation **Material of Construction**—Stainless Steel **Shell Size**—40" dia. × 30" height **Shell Plate Thickness**—3 mm **Bottom Plate Thickness**—5 mm **Lid Plate Thickness**—3 mm **Working Pressure**—2.5 kg/cm.sq. **Heating Arrangement**—Fire wood **Outlet Pipe**—S.S./Steam pipe (B Grade) 2"dia. and 36" length with valve. **Stack**—L shape 8"dia, M.S pipe 10" long ×18" L shape. **Grid**—46" × 46" (M.S squire rod 20 mm) 4" Pitch	0.5 m^3	—	50,000 to 60,000
2.	Rotatory	**Type**—Rotatory and Spherical Digester, Deshed and fitted with close type inlet **Material of Construction**—M.S. plate 10 mm thick and inside cladded with 2.0 mm S.S. plate or S.S. or S.S. Plate of 5-6 mm thick **Working Pressure**—2.0-2.5 kg/ cm^2 **Working Temperature**—100-120°C **Heating Arrangement**—Electrical with slip ring system **Drive System**—Reduction gear with electrical motors	0.5 m^3	3/5 HP with 9.0 kW heating elements	90,000 (M.S.) 1,50,000 (S.S.)
3.	Rotatory	**Type**—Rotatory and Spherical Digester, Deshed and fitted with close type inlet	1.5 m^3	5.0 HP	2,25,000 (M.S.) 3,25,000

S. No.	*Size of Machine*	*Details*	*Capacity*	*Req. HP*	*Appx. Cost (Rs.)*
		Material of Construction—M.S. Plate 10 mm thick and inside claided with 2 mm S.S. plate or S.S. plate of 5-6 mm thick. **Working Pressure**—2.0-2.5 kg/cm^2 **Working Temperature**—100-120°C **Heating Arrangement**—Steam heated **Drive System**—Reduction gear with electrical motor.			

TAUSOKI (PAPER DRYER)

S. No.	*Type*	*Details*	*Capacity*	*Req. HP*	*Appx. Cost (Rs.)*
1.	Stationary	**Type**—water heated **Shape**—rectangular **Plate Size**—30" × 40" **Material of Construction**—S.S. **Frame of MS Angle**—1"× 30"× 40" **S.S. (304) Polished Plates**—4 **Size**—30" × 40"× 2 mm thick **Size of Heating Column (with cover)**—Dia-2", Length—40", Thickness—6 to 8 mm **Thickness of Bottom Plates**—8 mm thick **Thickness of Upper Plates**—6 mm **Stack**—dia. 3" to 4", Height-6" **Platform**—M.S. 31"× 31" of 2" M.S. angle, Height 3", Grid having 10 mm dia. rod (M.S.)		—	30,000

PAPER MAKING VAT

S. No.	*Type*	*Details*	*Capacity*	*Req. HP*	*Appx. Cost (Rs.)*
1.	Autovat	**Material of Construction of Vat**—S.S. or M.S. with fabricated FRP coating of tank 42"× 56" teak wood with 1/2" angle frame **Size of Vat**—42"× 56" (inside) **Iron Strip Tradle**—1.5" and 3/8" • Function of treadle—to fix the deckle box of mould. The side ends are suspended by adjustable screws 1/4" rod 6" long to a common 1" rod. • Function of rod—to lift up and down the common angle iron pedal **Deckle** • Function of frame—to cover the mould inside. **Lower and Upper Deckle**—(wooden), Thickness—1/2" **Frame**—Wooden • Function of frame—to cover the mould with two side hinges. One end of frame is kept free to open the top frame to remove and insert the mould **Mould** • Size of mould—25" × 33"suitable for cut size paper of 22" × 30" **Frame**—(Teak Wood) • Breadth—1.5", Thickness—0.5" • The ribbed fabricated small wooden strips are fitted on back of frame. Supporting mesh—5 to 6 mesh S.S. wire	400 to 500 sheets/ shift	—	25,000 to 30,000

S. No.	*Type*	*Details*	*Capacity*	*Req. HP*	*Appx. Cost (Rs.)*
		• Top wire-stretched S.S. wire 40 mesh **Handles**—02 at each side (wooden) 2 Nos. each vat • Size of handle—26"× 33"			

PAPER CUTTING MACHINE

S. No.	*Type*	*Details*	*Capacity*	*Req. HP*	*Appx. Cost (Rs.)*
1.	Semi-automatic	**Blade Size**—42" with one spare knife **Material of Construction**— Main body—Cast Iron **Knives**—High carbon, High chromium	—	3HP 1440 rpm	60,000/- 75,000/-

CATEGORY OF THE UNITS

Type	*Capacity*
Tiny Unit	40 to 50 kg/day
Small Unit	100 to 150 kg/day
Medium Unit	250 to 300 kg/day
Large Unit	300 to 400 kg/day

Machinery and Equipment Required for Tiny Unit

Capacity —40 to 50 g. per day

TYPE OF PAPER MANUFACTURED FANCY AND DECORATIVE

S. No.	*Name of Machinery and Equipment*	*Capacity*	*HP Required*	*Approx Cost (Excluding Motor) in Rs.*
1.	Digester—stationary vomiting type for cooking (optional)	0.5 m	N.A.	50,000 to 60,000 each
2.	Hollander Beater—Portable Type Roll size : 16" × 20″	8-10 kg. per charge	5 H.P. Three Phase 960 rpm	70,000—75,000 M.S. 90,000-95,000 S.S.
3.	Paper Making Auto Vat/ Dipping Vat—1 No.	500-600 Sheets per shift	N.A.	25,000 to 30,000
4.	Screw Press (Manual Operated)	100-150 Sheets/cycle	N.A	40,000 to 45,000
5.	Tausuki (Paper Dryer) water heated, rectangular type S.S. and M.S. fabricated	500-600 Sheets/shift	N.A.	30,000 to 35,000
6.	Paper Cutting Machine (Manual)	—	N.A.	40,000 to 45,000
		Total	**5 H.P.**	**2,55,000 to 3,10,000**

Machinery and Equipment Required for Small Unit

Capacity: 100 to 150 kg. per day

TYPE OF PAPER MANUFACTURED FANCY AND DECORATIVE

S. No.	*Name of Machinery and Equipment*	*Capacity*	*HP Required*	*Approx Cost (Excluding Motor) in Rs.*
1.	Rag Chopper—8"-10" Blade size	50-60 kg./hr	3 H.P.	35,000
2.	Digester—stationary, vomiting type for cooking (optional)	0.05 m	N.A.	60,000
3.	Hollander Beater—Roll size: 18"× 24"	40-50 kg. per charge	10 H.P. Three Phase 960 rpm	95,000
4.	Paper making Auto Vat 2 Nos.	500-600 sheets per shift	N.A	30,000 × 2
5.	Screw Press (Motorized)	100-150 sheets/cycle	3 H.P.	70,000
6.	Tausuki (Paper Dryer) water heated, rectangular type S.S. and M.S. fabricated (optional)	500-600 sheets/shift	N.A.	30,000
7.	Calander Machine Roll size 9 "dia., 30"length	400-500 sheets/hr	3 H.P.	1,10,000
8.	Paper cutting machine—Blade (Size-automatic)	—	3 H.P.	80,000
		Total	**25 H.P.**	**4,50,000 to 5,40,000**

Machinery and Equipment Required for Medium Unit

Capacity: 250 to 300 kg. per day

TYPE OF PAPER MANUFACTURED—FANCY, DECORATIVE AND CARD SHEET

S. No.	*Name of Machinery and Equipment*	*Capacity*	*HP Required*	*Approx Cost (Excluding Motor) in Rs.*
1.	Rag Chopper—12" Blade size	80-100 kg./hr.	5 H.P.	50,000
2.	Hollander Beater—Roll size : 24" × 30"	80-100 kg./hr. per charge	15/20 H.P. Three Phase 960 rpm	1,25,000
3.	Paper Making Auto Vat 4 Nos.	500-600 sheets per shift	N.A.	30,000 × 4
4.	Hydraulic Press	60 M.T.	3 H.P.	1,60,000
5.	Calander Machine Roll size—12" dia., 36" length	500-600 sheets/hr	5 H.P.	1,70,000
6.	Paper Cutting Machine—Blade size 42" (Semi-automatic)	—	3 H.P.	75,000
		Total	**36 H.P.**	**7,00,000**

Machinery and Equipment Required for Large Unit

Capacity: 350 to 400 kg. per day

TYPE OF PAPER MANUFACTURED—FANCY, DECORATIVE AND CARD SHEET

S. No.	*Name of Machinery and Equipment*	*Capacity*	*HP Required*	*Approx Cost (Excluding Motor) in Rs.*
1.	Rag Chopper—14" Blade size	130 kg./hr	7.5 H.P.	60,000
2.	Hollander Beater—Roll size: face 30" × 36" dia.	130-140 kg per charge	25/30 H.P. Three Phase 960 rpm	1,60,000
3.	Paper Making Auto Vats. 6 Nos	500-600 sheets per shift	N.A.	30,000 × 6
4.	Hydraulic Press	100 M.T.	5 H.P.	1,90,000
5.	Calander Machine Roll size 12" dia., 36" length	500-600 sheets/hr	5 H.P.	1,70,000
6.	Paper Cutting Machine Blade size 42" (Semi-automatic)	—	3 H.P.	75,000
		Total	**10 H.P.**	**8,35,000**

Conclusion

Appropriate selection of the equipment is a key contributor to the delivery of asset performance when it is planned and implemented according to sound business drivers. It encompasses all aspects of human talent, machine expertise, correct assessment, well planned strategies engineering, practices, supply process, asset knowledge, machine improvement and continuous thriving for highest standards, so as to provide the greatest return on investment.

7

Research and Development Needs of Handmade Paper Industry

RAJESH PANT and ASHWINI KUMAR SHARMA

Introduction

Paper is an essential commodity, which is required by all walks of seciety. The consumption of paper is considered to be a yardstick of literacy and development of any society. Per capita consumption of paper in India one of the lowest in the world is about 5 kg., as a against that of the developed countries of around 300 kg. At present we produce about 5.5 million tonnes of paper in the organized sector. The production of handmade paper in the country is of the order of about 15,000 tonnes per annum coming out of about 400 handmade paper units. Although handmade paper can not come with mill made paper in many respects, for example scale of production, uniformity of quality etc., the paper produced in handmade paper sector has unique characteristics in many respects, for example many varieties of paper and products are special to this sector and can be developed in handmade paper sector only, thus making it superior to mill made paper.

The permanency of handmade paper is one such character, which is very important for its use for valuable documents, which are required to be preserved for long period. Further the handmade paper industry being cottage industry can provide employment to large number of people. On an average handmade paper making employees 1 person per tonne of annual production of handmade paper compared to much higher production per person in the organized sector. At present the handmade paper industry provides employment to over 18,000 persons mostly from rural areas. Wages earned by these workers are to the tune of over 20 crores, which is direct benefit to the majority of rural artisans. Female employment being 35 per cent of the total. Thus this industry is playing a very important role in the direction of poverty alleviation.

The production of handmade paper and board during the year 2003 has been around 15,000 tonne with a capacity utilization of around 55 per cent. Further the optimistic projected demand by the year 2010 had been of the order of 28,000 tonne. This indicates that there is a need to launch a programme by laying emphasis either on efficient capacity utilization or by creating additional capacity. Further, it is also necessary to identify alternative sources of raw materials to produce specialized quality of papers. Industry will also need technological up-gradation to meet the additional demand. The area of technological back up which could be provided by R&D institutes are described in the following part.

Identification of Alternative Raw Materials for Handmade Paper

With increasing demand and production of handmade paper, the most widely utilized and conventional cotton fibres would become expensive as well as scarce. It would be pertinent to make use of a variety of locally available alternative fibres. Each of these fibres has its own characteristics. A variety of products can be made out of these products either singly or in blend with other fibres.

KNHPI has made extensive efforts in this direction and have identified and developed technology for handmade paper production from number of such fibres. Some of the important fibres studied are listed in Table 7.1.

Table 7.1: Alternative Raw Materials for Handmade Paper

Common Name	*Botanical Name*
Shogum	*Daphne Papyracea.*
Pineapple	*Ananas Comosus merr.*
Sunn Hemp	*Crotolaria Juncea*
Silk Mulberry	*Moru Alba*
Bhimal	*Grewia Oppositifolia Roxb.*
Sisal	*Agabve Sisalina*
Ankara	*Calotropis Procera*
Sabai Grass	*Eulaliopsis Binata Linn.*
Banana	*Musa Sapientum*
Jute	*Corchorus Capsularis*

Some of these fibres, which are available in large quantities in various parts of the country are suitable for producing special types of papers and could be exploited for producing quality handmade papers.

There is a need to establish the use of these fibres by actual demonstration of the process under industrial conditions. Banana and jute fibres have already been established and are being used to some extent by the industry for producing speciality papers.

Efforts are being made in collaboration with industry to establish the use of other fibres as well.

Environmentally Compatible Process Technologies

At present point of time the industrial environmental pollution is one of the major concerns. Although handmade paper industry is considered to be eco-friendly as it uses very little or no chemicals and size of the individual units is small, which are generally scattered in wide areas. Whatever small pollution is generated is assimilated by the environment and its effect is not being felt. However, in the long run with increase in production the problem may magnify especially when the raw materials other than rags are used and with more use of chemicals in the papers etc. Further the pollution control may become stringent in near future. Therefore in order to retain the eco-friendly credentials of handmade paper, it is necessary to pay adequate attention to the environmental aspects of handmade paper manufacture.

Further to satisfy the environment conscious customers all over the world who demand eco-friendly products and to boost the export of handmade paper, it would have to be ensured that environment friendly process technologies are employed by making concerted efforts in the following areas.

- Application of Environment friendly pulping processes techniques
- Biotechnological Applications
- Energy conservation by process modifications
- Use of organic or vegetable dyes in place of synthetic dyes
- Use of recycled fibres for common varieties of papers
- Development of simple and cost effective effluent treatment system.

Application of Environmental Friendly Techniques in Pulping Process

Cotton rags, the conventional raw material for handmade paper industry does not require any chemicals for pulping. However, in the case of alternative raw materials, use of pulping chemicals mainly caustic soda is essential. In future the use of such raw materials is expected to increase. In the normal case, this may result in increased pollution due to pulping. Hence, there is a need to develop and propagate chemicals and simple process technologies with minimum adverse impact on the environment. In this context detailed studies have been conducted at KNHPI on applicability of following pulping processes for pulp production for handmade paper:

- Alkaline Peroxide Pulping
- Urea Pulping
- Neutral Oxalate Pulping
- Oxygen Pulping

Out of these alkaline peroxide pulping process has been found to be most promising with respect to pulp and paper qualities, as well as environmental reasons. The process is being used industrially for pulping of banana fibres. This further needs to be propagated for other fibres as well.

Biotechnological Applications

Application of biotechnology in pulp and paper industry has immense potential. Due to small scale of operation in handmade paper industry biopulping and biobleaching of raw materials for handmade paper would be quite appropriate. Similarly use of biological means of retting of bast and leaf fibres like jute, Kenaf, Ankara etc. needs to be explored. In this context, systematic studies have been initiated at KNHPI on bleaching and enzymatic retting. Encouraging results have been obtained in the case of bleaching of banana and other fibres with the use xylanese enxymes, which has resulted in reduction in bleaching chemicals and improvement in paper properties.

Energy Conservation Studies

Energy Conservation during Fibre Preparaion

Stock preparation consists of beating and refining of pulp to fibrillate the fibre bundles in order to increase this cellulose water reaction *i.e.* fibre swelling and hence, the strength development. This process in the handmade paper industry is being carried out in the Hollander Beater. The power consumption in beaters for handmade paper units using hosiery waste is extremely high *i.e.* in the range of 1.0-1.5 kWh/kg. of pulp. Study of fibre cutting and fibrillation of rag pulp or any other base fibres is critical to reduce the cost of the production of rags containing papers. There is scope for reducing the energy requirement. Studies are therefore needed for modification in the beating equipments as well as in the process of beating. This would ensure proper capacity utilization, energy saving and improved product quality.

In this context, studies carried out at KNHPI have shown that simple modifications in the process of beating could lead to about 20 per cent energy saving. This also results in improved pulp quality as well as higher production. Modification in design of the equipment may result in further improvement in the productivity. Efforts are therefore needed in this direction.

Process Machinery Modifications

There is a need to explore the possibilities of incorporating improvements in the unit process as well as in the machinery and equipment to improve the efficiency and uniformity of the product quality. This should be done by simple and cost effective devices that could be retrofitted into the existing system to obtain uniform product quality.

Control Device in Sheet Formation System

Large variation in grammage and thickness of the sheet is a common draw back of handmade paper. To maintain the uniformity the stock consistency needs to be maintained and stock sufficiently stirred before lifting the mould from the vat. To address this problem retrofitting of some devices to control consistency needs to be considered.

Improved Drying of Handmade Paper

Improved and efficient drying systems with low energy inputs for paper sheets needs to be designed. The studies could be directed in the following areas:

- Introduction of Taosuki for drying of fancy and decorative papers by utilizing low cost fuels, like locally available bio mass and other waste materials would ensure energy saving and waste utilization
- Development of hot air drying chambers to ensure that the production in the units does not suffer due to weather conditions.
- Designing of improved drying chambers with natural air circulation would ensure the energy efficient drying of the papers.

The possibility of setting up demonstration plant in some of the handmade paper units with above ideas may help the handmade paper industry.

Use of Vegetable Dyes

In the present day scenario, when people are becoming more and more environment conscious, there is a need to evaluate each and every aspect of manufacturing process for its eco-friendliness. Handmade paper industry uses synthetic dyes in the manufacture of coloured papers. These dyes have the possibility of containing azo group which release harmful emissions, which are allergic and carcinogenic in nature. European countries like Germany have banned the use of azo dyes. Hence, there is need to evaluate natural dyes for use in handmade paper.

Use of Recycled Fibres in Handmade Paper

In the common varieties of paper, it is desirable to use suitable quality of recycled fibre along with superior fibres like rags or bast to produce high quality eco-friendly product. The Institute has initiated work on the development of paper for card sheets. The paper could have properties comparable to that from 100 per cent rag pulp with better stiffness. Some preliminary results are shown in Table 7.2.

Table 7.2: Strength Characteristics of Handmade Paper for 50 per cent RCF for Card Sheets

S. No.	*Physical Properties*	*Paper Made from 100% Cotton Pulp*	*Paper Made from 50% Cotton Pulp + 50% Waste Paper Pulp*	*Paper Made from 100% Waste Paper Pulp*
1.	Basis weight (GSM)	194	218	227
2.	Tearing Index (Nm/gm)	12.61	18.53	11.93
3.	Tensile Index-(Nm/gm)	22.6	24.0	5.5
4.	Burst Index -Kpam$^{2/}$gm	1.804	2.38	0.792
5.	Folding Endurance	5884	9505	9
6.	Stiffness, Taber	17	15	9

Development of Effluent Treatment System for Handmade Paper Industry

Industrial environmental pollution is one of the major concerns all over the world. Although handmade paper industry is considered to be eco-friendly, even then with the increase in production and use of chemicals concentration of pollutants on the effluents is on the increase. The industry uses on an average 100 litres of water per kg. of paper produced. Depending on the production of paper water generated varies from 3.6-20.13 M^3 /day, which is being discharged without any treatment. Analysis of waste water in some cases were found to contain pollutants in excess of permissible limits. There is therefore need to monitor and check the pollutants in the discharged waste water and develop a cost effective technology for treatment of these effluents.

Quality Aspects of Handmade Paper

Export of handmade paper and its products is an important area. In the year 2002-03 country exported handmade paper and board worth Rs. 333 million. This has a potential to grow by at least 4.5 per cent per annum. Concerted efforts are needed in this direction. There is going to be tough competition in the coming years from the countries like Nepal, China, Thailand etc. who are making continuous efforts to improve the quality of their products. Therefore our producers will have to pay adequate attention to the quality and quality control aspects of handmade paper and its products. Compared to some of the handmade paper producing countries in Asia, our papers rank lower in some quality aspects. Indian handmade paper is generally poor in quality when compared to those of Europe, Japan, Korea etc. Some of these quality aspects, which need careful attention, are described below:

- **Cleanliness**—This problem is mainly on account of raw material, which need to be cleaned thoroughly by dedusting after cutting or sorting. The equipment like beaters and beaters and vats should also be cleaned after days work. The chemicals like starch etc. used for surface sizing should be screen properly and sizing should be done in clean room.

- **Variation in grammage and thickness**—Large variation in substance is a common drawback. To maintain the uniformity, the stock consistency must be maintained and stock sufficiently stirred before lifting the mould from the vat.
- **Variation in shade whiteness and colour**—Some times there is large variation in whiteness of sheets and colour from one consignment to other. In order to achieve consistency, operation should be properly controlled, for example use of measured quantity of chemicals etc.
- **Variation in formation**—Since handmade paper is made out of long fibres the formation is relatively poor. To improve this fibre should be properly processed for good fibrillation as well as fibre cutting. Further formation aids (defloculations) should be reused. These could be synthetic or vegetable mucilages. There is a need to identify defferent mucilages and grade them on the basis of viscosity, *p*H, temperature, shelf life, efficiency and reactivity with the fibres.
- **Print defects**—For printing papers bulk and opacity are two main requirements. They should be taken care of by proper sizing and loading.
- **Acidity in paper**—This is mainly due to alum used in sizing, which reduces the life of the paper. For making permanency papers, neutral sizing and tub sizing with gelatine is necessary.
- **Sorting of sheets**—Proper attention needs to be paid for sorting of defective sheets. A mechanism of sheet inspection before packaging must be introduced especially for export consignment.
- **Poor packing**—A well packed ream of paper looks more attractive. The packaging must be dimensioned and sizes printed prominently for easy identification.

Uniformity of the product specially with respect to grammage, thickness is an essential requirement where there is a considerable scope for improvement. Therefore need for technical audit and modification and standardization of various machineries used specially in the area of beating. Sheet formation and calandering of the sheets.

Standardization of Handmade Paper Products

Indian handmade paper industry is basically based on cotton hosiery waste and waste papers. Use of locally available cellulosic fibres is also being used to limited extent. Presently variety of papers are made by the handmade paper units, which can be grouped into:

- Card varieties
- Stationary, fancy and decorative varieties
- Tissue papers
- Industrial varieties
- Packaging and wrapping papers

A good number of units in the country are engaged in producing varieties of handmade paper and paper products without considering the end use of the products. Number of handmade paper varieties, which are listed above are in the market without having any standard specifications.

Customers require products with characteristics, which satisfy their needs and expectations. These in term are expressed as product specification, which may be referred to as customer requirements. Therefore, in case of handmade paper to satisfy the customers and avoid any complaints as well as to maintain the uniformity of the products produced at different units, it may be essential to have a code of special specifications. This would ensure the production of quality product with sustained supply to the customers. It is therefore worthwhile to consider the formulation of specifications for at least those varieties of handmade papers, which are most in demand. Formation of standards of such varieties would ensure the uniformity of the quality of these products produced by different units. At present only handmade drawing paper and filter paper have the BIS specifications.

In the past KNHPI had initiated work in this direction of formulating standard specifications for following four varieties of handmade paper and board.

- Writing and printing papers
- Packaging papers
- Papers for shopping bags
- Paper for file covers

The work was conducted by reviewing the BIS specifications related to pulp and paper, preparation of large number of paper samples of above mentioned varieties of handmade papers in the laboratories and pilot plants and testing these for various strength and optical properties. Analysis of data based on these the draft of the specifications arrived at have been compiled.

It is recommended that BIS should be associated in this so that further plan of action could be worked out in consultation with the industry.

Conclusions

In the handmade paper sector continuous R and D efforts are needed in the following areas:

- Exploration and identification of locally available and easy pulpable ligno-cellulosic raw materials for handmade paper industry and establish their use in the industry.
- Development of compatible process technologies for handmade paper production, to maintain the environment friendly credential of handmade paper industry.

- Process and machinery modifications, to conserve energy and other utilities and improve the productivity.
- Development of simple and techno economically viable effluent treatment system of handmade paper units.

In addition to above, efforts may also be required to develop product specifications for some common varieties of handmade papers, in order to maintain the uniformity of the products in different units.

8

Eco-Friendliness of Handmade Paper
Application of Natural Dyes

SAAKSHY AGARWAL

Introduction

It will not be exaggeration to say that today handmade paper has emerged as one of the prominent sector in export market. The sector is spreading its feathers and this can be visibly seen by increasing demand and production of handmade paper in domestic as well as in export market. As the world is becoming more environment conscious the obsession for handmade paper is increasing day by day. So its use creates a sense of our credibility to our environment along with pleasing our visual sense. Alarming environment problems has shaken the world to think about our environment before it is too late. Fortunately, developed countries has taken a step forward and set norms at manufacturing/product making/user's end for their environment friendliness. Handmade paper not the exemption has also to prove its eco-friendliness in terms of certain criteria satisfying its eco-friendliness as given below:

- Use of non-woody raw material
- Eco-friendly pulping process
- Eco-friendliness of paper after addition of chemical additives
- Non-polluting process.

The eco-friendliness of handmade paper includes nature of dyes, acidity/alkalinity of paper and presence of azo group in dye.

In the present milieu, concern for the environment has created an escalating interest in natural dyes. It is common belief that natural dyes are more friendly to the environment than synthetic dyes. Moreover, when the question of fastness is raised, it is to note that all museum textiles predating 1856 are naturally dyed. Even after so many years their colours remain rich, vibrant, beautiful and inspiring. Dyes which were in use in Greco-Roman times and in the Middle Ages were almost entirely natural dyes. In India, the most important mineral pigments analyzed from paintings on walls, cloth and paper have been natural dyes. The depictions on wall paintings of Ajanta, Ellora and other sites indicate that early Indian very well knew dyeing and painting on fabric. The dyers, printers as well as ayurvedic practitioners with their vast experience and skill have contributed much to natural dyes. They tried each and every part of plants like roots, heartwood, branches, leaves, flowers, pods, buds, fruits etc. In spite of tremendous efforts, it has been felt that little scientific advancement has been made in vegetable dyes. The reason might be advent of synthetic dyes after 1856 dominated the world trade of colours and substituted vegetable dyes to a very good extent. The use of vegetable dyes continued only in few pockets of India as a small industry.

Dyes

Dye is very important aspect in handmade papermaking. A simple method of applying dyes to cotton fibres involves the dissolution of dye in water and then adding the filtered solution of dye to fibre suspension in beater. Since dyeing is done directly on cotton dyes belonging to this class is called direct dye. In handmade paper making the conventional dye used is direct dye due to its more fastness to light and strong affinity for cellulose.

What is Fastness to Light?

When a dyed paper is exposed to sunlight during its drying or use, the dye should not fade or change its colour that shows good fastness to light. During exposure to sunlight the dye absorbs some portion of sunlight, the absorbed light has certain amount of energy and the absorbed energy may bring out self-destruction of the dye in the presence of oxygen and moisture. Instrument named as Xenon Arc tester is used to evaluate the fastness to light.

What are Azoic Dyes?

Direct dyes having azo group (-N=N-) are called azoic dyes. Azo dyes release harmful amines which are allergic, carcinogenic or poisonous in nature. Germany is very specific about the use of Azo-dyes which on reduction release carcinogenic or harmful amines. Twenty-two harmful amines are found so far by Germany. Germany was the first country to impose a comprehensive ban on presence of azo dyes containing harmful amines or which are reduced to carcinogenic aryl amines. Many other countries followed this ban. The benzidine based dyes was stopped in almost all countries to stop workers from coming in contact with cancer using Benzidene. The presence of banned amines is analyzed with the help of Gas chromatography.

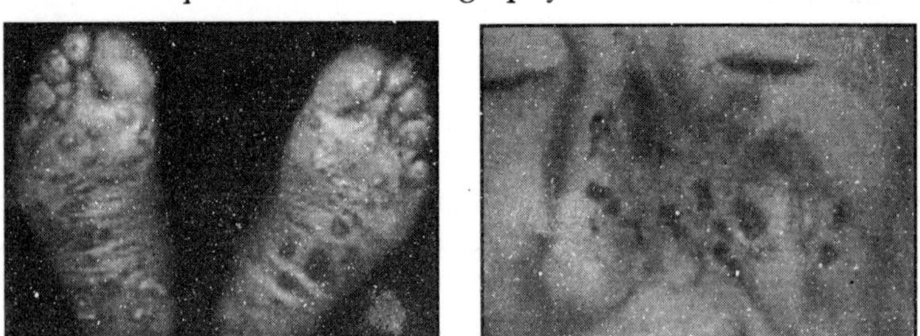

Fig. 8.1: Photos showing skin cancer

For safety evaluation of the dermal exposure of consumers to azo dyes from wearing coloured textiles, a possible cleavage of azo dyes by the skin micro flora should be considered since, in contrast to many dyes, aromatic amines are easily absorbed by the skin. The 22 amines used in azo dyes and reported by German scientists, to be harmful are as given in Table 8.1. The other dyes which have been reported to be toxic are given in Table 8.2.

Table 8.1: List of Harmful Amines

4,4′-methylene-bis-(2 chloroaniline)	3,3′-Dichloro benzidine
2-methoxy aniline	*p*-amino azo-benzene
4-Amino diphenyl	*p*-Kresidine
4-chloro-*o*-toluidine	4,4′-oxydianiline
2-Napthylamine	3,3′-Dimethyl-benzidine
p-chloroaniline	3,3′-Dimethyl-4,4′-diaminodiphenyl methane
2,4-Diamino anisole	4,4′-Thiodianiline
4,4′-Diamino diphenyl methane	*o*-Toluidine
2,4-Diamino toluene	2,4,5-Trimethyl aniline
O-amino azo toluene	2-amino-4-nitro toluene
Benzidine	3,3′-Dimethoxy benzidine

A study was conducted by collecting the representative sample of coloured handmade paper from different handmade paper units and evaluated for the nature of dyes including presence of azo group.

The results showed that all handmade paper samples have been dyed with direct dyes. It was found that a specific shade has got more possibility of having azo group in comparison to others.

Table 8.2: Toxic Dyes with Their Lethal Dosage Concentration

		LD50Mg/kg	*Irritation Skin (Rabbit)*	*Irritation Eye (Rabbit)*
Basic Blue 7	CI 42595	100	–	+
Basic Blue 81	CI 42598	205	–	+
Basic Red 12	CI 48070	25	–	+
Basic Violet 16	CI 48013	90	–	+
Basic Yellow 21	CI 48060	171	–	+

History of Natural Dyes

The history of natural dyes is very interesting. The earlier written record of the use of natural dyes was found in China dated 2600 BC. Chemical tests of red fabrics in the tomb of King Tutankhamen in Egypt show the presence of alizarin, a pigment extracted from madder. Alexander the great had deceived the Persians in to thinking that his army was wounded by sprinkling his soldiers with red dye, probably madder juice which contains the dye alizarin.

The first fibre dyes were already used in pre-historic times after the last ice age around 1000 BC. They consisted of fugitive stains from berries, blossoms, barks and roots. The earliest written record of the use of natural dyes was found in China dated 2600 BC. Chemical tests of red fabrics in the tomb of king Tutankhamen in Egypt show the presence of alizarin, a pigment extracted from madder. In the more modern times, Alexander the great had deceived the Persians into thinking that his army was wounded by sprinkling his soldiers with a red dye, probably madder juice, which contains the dye alizarin.

Natural dyes are dyestuffs made from plants, minerals, and in the case of cochineal, an insect. Some of natural dyes are Indigo (Indigoferatinctoria Linn.), Indian Madder (Rubia cordifolia), Henna (Lawsoniainermis), Catechu (Acacia catechu), Ratanjot (Ornosmas Echioides), Tesu (Buteamonsperma Lam.Kuntze), Myrobalan (Terminaliache-bula), Tamarind (Tamarindus indica Linn.), Safed kikar (Acacia leucophloea wild.) etc. No doubt, natural dyes in comparison to direct dyes are more trouble and take longer to prepare. Some of the chemical colours (direct dyes) are not fast to light and washing but natural dyes as madder, lichens, catechu etc. are fast. Natural dyes have limited range of shades in comparison to synthetic dyes so lot of study is needed on evaluation of maximum possible shades.

Dyes and Their Source

Table 8.3: Natural Dyes

S.No.	*Botanical name*	*Local name*	*Source*
1.	*Punica granatum Linn.*	Anar	Rind of pomegranate
2.	*Indigofera tinctoria Linn.*	Indigo	Leaves
3.	*Terminalia chebula*	Harda	Fruit
4.	*Acacia catechu*	Kutch, Khayer, Katha	Bark
5.	*Terminalia arjuna*	Arjun	Bark
6.	*Kerria Lacca*	Lac	Secretion of Kerria Lacca on host plant Palas
7.	*Rubia cordifolia Linn.*	Indian madder Manjishtha	Root of Madder
8.	*Eucalyptus comaldulensis*	Eucalyptus	Leaves
9.	*Lantana*	Lantana dye	Leaves
10.	*Lawsonia inermis Linn.*	Henna	Leaves
11	*Buteamonosperma(Lam) Kuntze*	Tesu flower	Flower
12	*Pterocarpusnsantalinus Linn.*	Chandan	Bark of Chandan
13	*Acacia Arabica*	Babul	Bark of Babul

Natural Dyes Obtained from Plants

Indigofera tinctoria

It is a substantive dye, which is different from any other dye as it does not require any mordant, yet the colour achieved is extremely fast to washing and to light. Rather, it is dyed through a living fermentation process. Slowly the air changes it to the beautiful deep and rich blue of Indigo, which is having good light fastness. The leaves of Indigofera tinctoria plant are fermented in fermentation pits. The dye is precipitated by oxidation or by passing the air. The precipitated blue natural dye at bottom is dried in the air to make the cake. The appearance of dye is blue and main colouring compound is Indigotin.

Terminalia chebula

The dried fruits of "Terminalia chebula" (Myrobalan) is used to produce the dye. The appearance of dye powder is brown and the main colouring component is chebulinic acid. It is used in Ayurvedic preparations and has therapeutical value.

Quercus infectoria

The gallnuts of Quercus infectoria are pulverized to required particle size and extracted in aqueous media. The extract is filtered and spry in vacuum dryer to obtain the dye. Quercus infectoria is dried secretion of an insect living on the tree. The main colouring component is Gallotannic acids and appearance of dye powder is brownish yellow.

Acacia catechu

The cutch is used as raw material for manufacturing the dye, which is obtained from the left over of katha produced from Acacia catechu. Katha is used as edible paste in pan preparations. The main colouring component is Catechin/Flavanoid.

Rubia cordifolia

It is contained in the roots of the madder plant. The plants are dug up, the roots washed, dried and ground into powder. It is found beneath the outer bark of the roots when the plants are about three years old. At this age, the roots of the plant render a suitable dye. Only about two per cent dye is obtained from the dried roots. The madder named as "Turkey Red" was very popular during 19th century.

Terminalia arjuna

The bark and dried fruits of Terminalia arjuna is used for manufacturing the dye. The dry bark from the stem contains 15-24 per cent tannin and used in tanneries.

Tectona grandis

The dye is produced from dried leaves of Teak tree. The main colouring compound in the dye is Tectoleafquinone.

Fig. 8.2: Indigo

Fig. 8.3: Harad

Fig. 8.4: Quercus infectoria

Fig. 8.5: Katha

Fig. 8.6: Arjuna

Fig. 8.7: Manjishtha

Natural Dyes Obtained from Animals

Cochineal

It is an important red element for the natural dye user. It is the brightest of all the available natural red dyes. This dye is found in the cochineal louse, which feeds on cactus plants. The female insect is dried in sun and grounded to produce a rich red powder. The yield under the best conditions is about 2.72 kgs. per acre of cacti.

Kerria Lacca

The dye is obtained as a byproduct of the secretion of insect Kerria Lacca. The main colouring component is Laccaic acid.

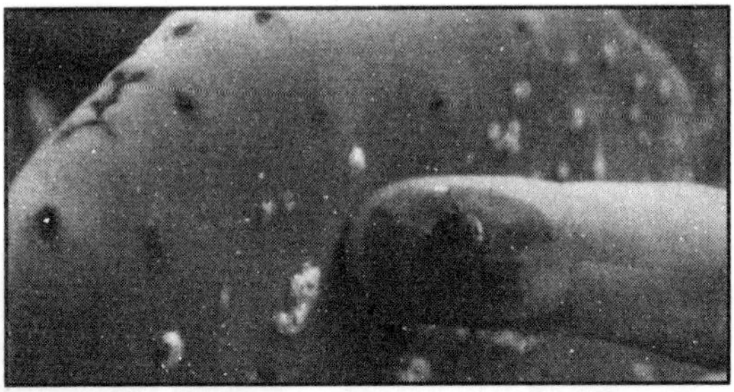

Fig 8.8: Secretion of cochineal insect on cactus plant

Natural Dyes Obtained from Minerals

Cinnabar (Hindi:Sangarf)
Red lead (Sindur)
Red ochre (Geru)
Ultramarine (Lajwad)
Zinc white (Safeda)

Mineral dyes are obtained from an impure earthy ore of iron or ferruginous clay, usually red or yellow. Some of the most important mineral pigments used in India as analyzed from paintings on walls, cloth and paper have been Cinnabar (Hindi:Sangarf), Red lead (Sindur), Red ochre (Geru), Ultramarine (Lajwad), Zinc white (Safeda), Yellow ochre (Ram Raj).

Yield of Natural Dyes

Yield of some of the natural dyes are as given below:

Table 8.4: Yield of Natural Dyes

S.No.	*Dye*	*Source*	*Dye Content,%*
1.	Madder	Root bark	1.9
2.	Cochineal	Female cochineal louse	1.8
3.	Indigo	Indigo plant leaves	1.5-2.0
4.	Saffron	Crocus plant flower pistil	7.0
5.	Annatto	Roucone- tree seed	15.0
6.	Carotin	Carrot, red palm oil, pumpkin seed	<0.5
7.	Lac	Stick lac	0.5-0.75

Table 8.5: Characteristics of some purified natural dye powders

Botanical name	*Common name*	*Moisture*	*Water-soluble matter (%)*	*pH of 1% solution*	*Ash (%)*
Acacia Catechu	Cutch	6.0	95.0	6.0	7.0
Rubia cordifolia	Indian madder	5.0	95.0	8.0	35.0
Terminalia chebula	Myrobolan	5.0	97.0	3.5	7.0
Indigofera tinctoria	Indigo	5.0	4.0	5.0	63.0

Classification of Natural Dyes

First classification of natural dyes was according to alphabetical order. Later classification based on chemical structure, where grouping with in each structure class according to hue was carried out. In colour index, the dyes were classified according to chemical composition as well as major application classes. The natural colour and hue of a dye can be altered by treating with metal salts. The colour of dye originated from plant depends on soil properties, part of plant, and season of harvesting, cultivation practices etc.

Chemical Class

The natural organic dyes and pigments cover a wide range of chemical classes *viz.* ketone, anthroquinonoids, napthoquinones, flavones, indigoids and chlorophyll.

Indigoid Dyes

Indigo perhaps the oldest natural dye used by man occurs as the glucoside indicant in the plant Indigofera tinctoria. It is an example of vat dye.

Anthroquinone Based Dyes

Some of the most important red dyes are based on the anthroquinone structure. They are obtained both from plants as well as insects or animals. These dyes are characterized by good fastness to light. They form complexes with metal salts and the resultant metal complex dyes have good wash fastness.

Madder dyes are hydroxyl-anthroquinones which are extracted from the root bark of various Rubiaceae *e.g.* from madder root (Rubia tinctorum). The roots contain approximately 1.9 per cent of dye present in the free form or bound as the glucoside. Madder also known as alizarin was the first natural dye to be synthesized chemically in 1869.

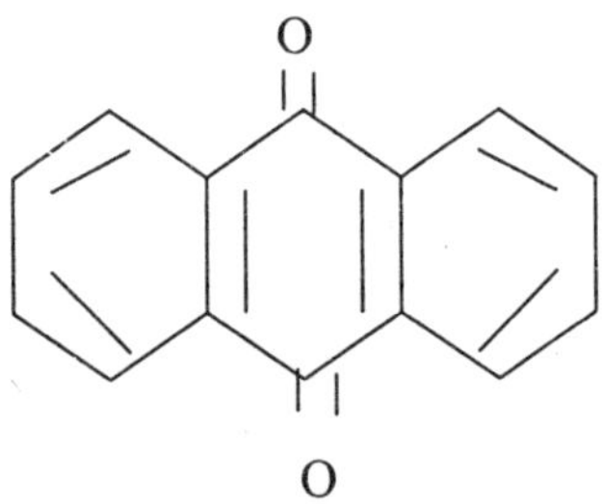

Anthroquinone structure

Lac Dye

Lac is probably the most ancient of the animal dyes. It has been used in Southeast Asia and India since the beginning of the recorded history. The dye yields scarlet and crimson shades which exhibit good properties, especially to light and washing. Structurally, the principal colouring component has been identified as laccaic acid.

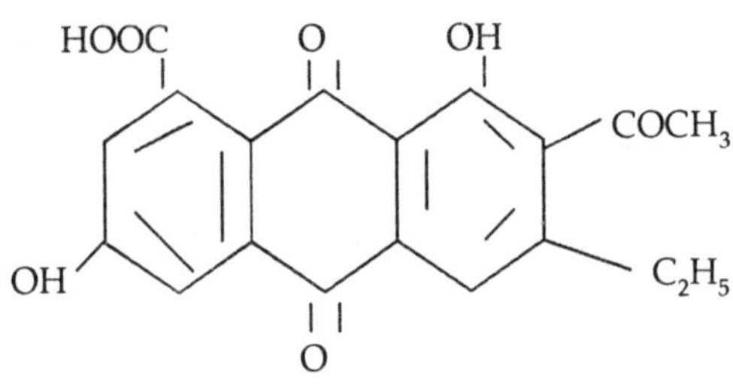

Laccaic acid

Cochineal

Cochineal is obtained from an insect of the same name which feeds on the cactus plant. Chemically cochineal is similar to kermenes. The main colouring component of this dye is carminic acid.

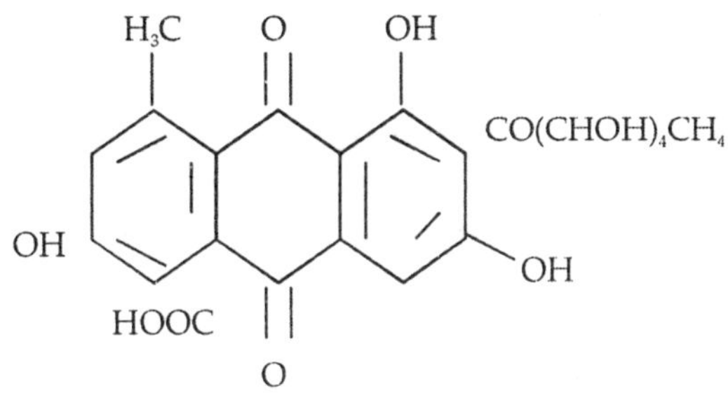

Carminic acid

Alpha-Naphthoquinones

The most prominent member of this class of dyes is Lawsone inermis or Henna. It is obtained from the leaves of Lawsonia inermis, cultivated mainly in India and Egypt. Lawsone has been identified as 2-hydroxy-1-4-napthoquinone. Another similar dye is Juglone, 5-hdroxy-1-4-napthoquinone obtained from the shells of unripe walnuts.

Application of Classes of Natural Dyes

Natural dyes were classified in two groups, namely substantive and adjective dyes by Bancroft in his "Treatise on Permanent colours". According to this classification the dyes such as indigo orchid turmeric etc. which dye the fibres directly are classified as substantive dyes, while adjective dyes only dye material mordant with metallic salt, examples of such dyes are logwood, madder, cochineal, fustic etc. in pure state the adjective dyes are generally only slightly coloured and when used alone they give poor dyeing.

Mordant Dyes

Dyes having affinity for the mordanted fibres or which form a complex with the mordant are called mordant dyes. The complex may be formed by first applying the mordant or by simultaneous application of the mordant and the dye or by after treatment of the dyed material. For a dye to be called as mordant dye, it should have electron donating groups capable of forming complex with the transition metal salts.

Alizarin was perhaps the first mordant dye. This dye has no affinity for cotton, however on mordanting with a metal salt such as alum it is readily absorbed by the fibre.

Vat Dyes

Vat dyes derive their name from the wooden fermentation vessel called the vat which was at one time used for reducing the dye and converting it into soluble form. The process of solubilisation of the dye is known as vatting.

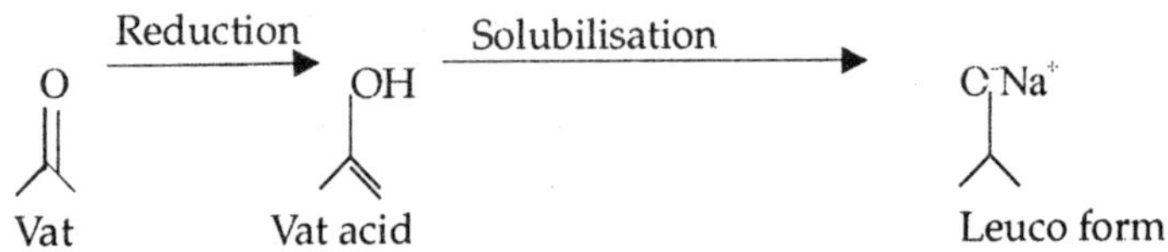

The soluble form of the dye is called leuco dye. The leuco form of the dye is not only soluble in water but has affinity for the natural fibres. The vatting of indigo can also be carried out by treatment with a reducing agent, such as sodium hydrosulphite and an alkali such as sodium hydroxide. The leuco or the reduced form of the dye is oxidized back to the original form on keeping the dyed material for 15-20 minutes at room temperature before washing. The true colour is produced on treatment with hot soap solution.

Experimental Work and Results

The samples of commercially available natural dyes were procured. Application of natural dyes using cotton rags as raw material has been explored. The conventional dye *i.e.* direct dye was compared with natural dye to explore suitability of natural dyes in handmade paper sector. Pulp of cotton rags beaten up to 300 ml freeness level and dye of 1 per cent concentration was prepared for the study.

Evaluation of Spent Liquor

The waste spent liquor of natural dyes and direct dyes is evaluated for BOD (Biochemical Oxygen Demand) and COD (Chemical Oxygen Demand) which was determined with titration method. It has been found that BOD and COD of the effluent of natural dyes are far lower than that of direct dyes as given in Table 8.6

Table 8.6: Comparison of Effluent Parameters of Spent Liquor of Natural and Direct Dyes

Particulars	*Natural Dye (1%)*	*Direct Dye (1%)*
COD, ppm	800	2400
BOD, ppm	110	250

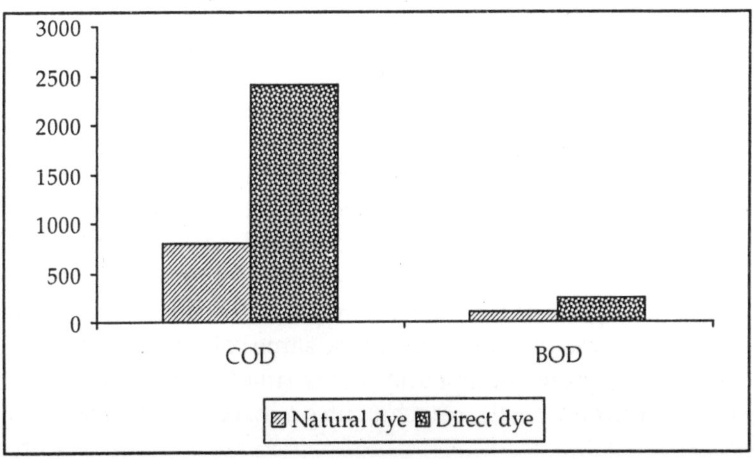

The above data clearly indicates the remarkable difference in COD and BOD values of effluent of dyes utilizing direct dyes and natural dyes. COD value of effluent of natural dye is approximately 65 per cent lower than that of effluent of direct dyes while BOD showed approximately 55 per cent lower value of effluent of natural dyes in comparison to effluent of direct dyes.

Evaluation of Light Fastness of Paper

The light fastness of paper dyed with natural and synthetic dyes were evaluated in terms of scale with the help of Xenon arc tester by exposing the sample for 24 hrs. The results of the same are as given in Table 8.7.

Table 8.7: Light Fastness of Natural and Direct Dyed Paper

S.No.	*Dye and the Form of Paper*	*Light Fastness*
1	Quercus Infectoria (Natural dye)	Scale 4
2	Quercus Infectoria, mordanted (Natural dye)	Scale 4
3	Quercus Infectoria, sized (Natural dye)	Scale 4
4	Rubia Cordifolia (Natural dye)	Scale 4
5	Pink, direct dye (Synthetic dye)	Scale 2
6	Pink, direct dye sized (Synthetic dye)	Scale 2

Higher the value of scale better the light fastness. Natural dyes showed twice better light fastness in comparison to direct dyes with the help of xenon arc tester.

Comparison of Synthetic Dyes and Natural Dyes

No doubt, natural dyes in comparison to direct dyes are more trouble and take longer to prepare. Direct dyes are not fast to light and washing but natural dyes are having very good fastness to light. When direct dyes fades it becomes a different colour and generally a bad one while when a natural colour fades it becomes a lighter tone of the same colour. Natural dyes are extracts from therapeutic plants (madder, indigo, Brazil wood, logwood, fustic, catechu/cutch), insects (cochineal) and naturally occurring minerals (alum, iron, tin) needed by body in trace amounts. Natural dyes have limited range of shades in comparison to synthetic dyes so a lot of study is needed on evaluation of maximum possible shades.

Conclusion

The study conducted on application of natural dyes in handmade paper making nullify the possibility of paper having azo group, thus enhancing the eco-friendly credentials of handmade paper making. This will boost export of Indian handmade paper in international market. Use of natural dyes in coloured handmade paper needs to be propagated to eliminate the possibility of presence of toxic azo group in the paper due to synthetic dyes. This would help in retaining the eco-friendly credentials of handmade paper.

REFERENCES

Cheryl Kolander, Master Natural Dyer, Aurora Silk, 1995.

Ethel Mairet M., Pepler D., A Book on Vegetable Dyes, 1916, Hampshire House Workshops, Hammersmith, Sussex, England.

Textile Committee, Mumbai, October 2001.

Saakshy, Sharma A.K., Application of Natural Dyes in Handmade paper making, Souvenir Indian Paper 2006,Vapi,10-13th November 2006.

9

Challenges in the Growth of HMP Industry and Scope of Use of Renewable Energy in its Manufacturing

N.K. ROY

Paper is one of the necessities of civilisation and growth and it is impossible to imagine its continuance without Printed Books and Newspapers. In fact the per capita consumption of Paper (Writing, News-prints, Wraping, Packaging etc.) is considered a good index of stage of progress of a nation. Judging by this yardstick, India is far behind the developed countries—as some data (of 90's) indicate as consumption of paper in USA 77297 (in thousand tonnes) was while in India during the corresponding period it was only 2182.

The origin of paper making is ascribed to T. Sain Hun, who presented it to Emperor Hai of China in A.D. 105. This paper was made from Vegetable fibre that had been well macerated so that each individual filament was a separate unit. The fibres were intermixed with water and the suspension poured over a silver like screen. The water drained through the small opening of the screen, leaving sheet of matted fibre upon the Screen's surface. This layer of inter laced fibre was lifted from the screen and dried—Rags of Cotton and linens were the main raw-materials for this method of HANDMADE PAPER, which continued till 1800.

With the invention of the Paper machine in 1798 in France, the supply of rags soon proved insufficient to meet the demand of increased paper production possible by machine making. The process of making mechanical Wood-Pulp was discovered in Germany and of making Chemical Wood pulp in 1855 in U.K. Coniferous Wood has since been the main raw-material for paper making in the World.

In India, the first commercial paper machine was installed in 1867. The raw-material used was mainly imported pulp. The suitability of Bamboo for making paper was established by the extensive investigation of W. Raott at Forest Research Institute (FRI), Dehradun from 1909 to 1925. The institute at a later stage established that it is possible to make acceptable paper from short-fibre hard woods by mixing some long fibre-pulp and suitably modifying the process. The rapid expansion of paper industry based on these two discoveries—gave a new boost to paper production on one hand and on the other hand became a serious cause of concern of felling of tree threateching our eco-systems and foresty.

Vision of Mahatma Gandhi—In the Context of Environment and Village Industries

Gandhi set two objectives for himself. A near term objective of Political Independence through the path of peaceful and passive struggle, and a long-term objective of economic Independence for India's teaming millions based on Social, Environmental, Equity, Cultural and ethical considerations. The former was achieved during his lifetime and the later is still a dream the nation is striving to achieve.

The present pattern of development poses serious threats to global ecosystem. In large areas of World, human claims on biological systems are reaching an unsustainable level. When this happens, fisheries collapse, forest disappear, grasslands are converted into barren waste lands and croplands deteriorate. According to one statistics, 100 acres of tropical forest are cut every one minute. In 40 years, if this trend continues, there would be no forest left.

The signal or alarm bell in this regard has already rung—when we in the recent past experienced a Tsumani—claiming 2-lakh human-lives and causing irrepairable damage to eco-system. The green-grass grown in Antarctica or snow-fall in Middle-east deserts—only indicate, how serious our future is going to become. What would be the fate of mankind, if as scientist predict the trend of environmental disaster continuous to be as it is now, the average temperature rise of the earth by next 20 years would increase by 20°C—due to green-house and other ecosystem deterioration.

Gandhiji, way back in 40's had said, "we can use the bounties of nature but not with an element of greed." He was a vegetarian and had compassion for all living objects. In fact he had said "man has no power to create life, therefore he has no right to kill life". In this context, there is an instructive story from the life of the Buddha. A hunter shot down a bird with an arrow and the injured bird fell in the lap of Buddha, who was meditating under the tree. Seeing the injured Bird in agony, Buddha healed it. The hunter came running and said that the Bird was his, because he had killed it. But Buddha replied, "the Bird is mine because, I gave it life," which is greater, taking life or giving life? In the larger context, which is greater act, looting, vandalizing, earth's bio-diversity and other resources or sustainably utilising these with manageable effect on the environment.

Gandhiji and Vinobaji "spoke for those who do not speak, to claim for those who claim noting, and for the poor who are waiting in silence for centuries". He realised that "the land will not be able to absorb all our people and other must turn to small scale Industry and Social Service. These thoughts brought the middle class intelligentsia and peasants nearer to each other. All this lead Gandhiji to propagate decentralised model of Rural development for over 5.76 lakh villages. Today the challenge before the nation is to make a creative synthesis between Gandhiji as model of bottom-up Rural development and Nehru is as model of top-down industrial development. The former leads to economy of permanence and is based—LARGELY ON RENEWABLES, where damage to environment is manageable, while the later is based largely on non-renewable and cause environmental pollution, and depollution is costly.

The above vision of Gandhiji, had lead Sri Kumarappa ji, to organise an all India Village-Industries movement—when by Handmade paper—making as an ancient traditional craft were taken up to be developed as an ancient employment generating activity when raw material inputs were wholly solely RENEWABLES AND WASTE. *The journey of its growth—is slow-paced but is absolutely in right direction-under patronage and nurturing of KVIC and one name which history of HMP—in this country will always remember is Dr. Kamal Taori—the CEO of KVIC in 1990-96, when new blood infusion and rejuvination measures to revamp the HMP industry were initiated by taking up for the first time on UNDO Project by KVIC which enabled exposure of the HMP sector for diversification to attract foreign market.*

SWOT Strength

Analysis of HMP-Industry—We may restrict our study to only strength and weakness areas relevant to the topic of discussion in this paper.

1. Use of Non-forest Material.
2. Environment friendly.
3. Low per capita investment.
4. High employment potential.
5. High percentage of Wages.
6. Cent percent indigenous machineries.
7. Relatively low energy and water consumption compared to mill-made paper.
8. Long durability.
9. Negligible or no chemical action on the fibre properties.
10. Immense export potential.
11. Low management cost.
12. Enables production of desired quality in any small or big quantity—as per need of market.
13. Fancy and decorative papers at affordable price.
14. Tremendous scope of diversification of product.
15. Product developments of value-added items by way of conversion—generating additional employment.

Weaknesses

1. Inadequate Technology for drying of Paper-board, sheet formulation etc.
2. Lack of professional skill in production and marketing.
3. Inadequate quality control.
4. Dearth of skilled workers.
5. Absence of aggressive marketing approaches.
6. Lack of publicity.
7. Reach of technology in select pocketed areas.

An Outline of Manufacturing Process

Preliminary operations: Raw-material treatment includes cutting, shorting, dusting of raw-materials. The raw-material should be carefully sorted and thoroughly screened and dusted, before beating. If agro-waste is raw-material-input, a digesting of raw-material is required:

Equipment/Appliances used: Rag-chopper, Digester, Washing drum etc.

Beating: The pulp needs to be well beaten free from knots and lumps. However excessive and prolong beating should be avoided. It should be thoroughly washed by washing drum before wet-beating. Maximum care should be taken to clean the bed plate on completion of each beating cycle. The pulp should be bleached carefully depending on the degree of whiteness desired.

Equipment/Appliance: Hollander-beater etc.

Lifting, Pressing and Drying: (1) The pulp should be thoroughly stirred maintaining low consistency before lifting for uniform formation. If any foreign materials or lumps are noticed, they should be removed. While lifting proper shake should be given for orientation of fibres in all directions.

(2) The felt/napkins should be thoroughly washed and cleaned and not allowed to drop to get soiled, to avoid adherence of dirt, dust and other particles or stains on the body of the paper.

(3) The wet sheets should be pressed in hydraulic or screw press for enough time to obtain stiffness and compactness.

(4) Moulds should not be kept during lifting or after use at pleaces where dirt and dust are likely to come in contact with. They should be thoroughly washed before use.

(5) The wet sheets after pressing should be loft dried. They should not be spread on the ground for drying as many units practise, otherwise they would be impregnated with dirt, dust and other foreign materials. Napkins and felts will also pick up such unwanted things which will be embedded in the body of paper during lifting.

Peeling and Sorting: Rigorous sorting should be done after drying. The sheets not found up to the mark and those having any defects should be outright rejected and sent back to beating section for recycling.

Surface Sizing: The paper should be hard surface sized with starch or glue to avoid tacky ink or loose fibres on the surface. After sizing the paper should be sorted and sorted again and only good sheets should be allowed to move to the glazing section.

Calendering: The sheets should be well calendered for smoothness and glaze. On demand, various types of finishes like medium, linen, etc., can be imparted.

Some Critical Issues of HMP—Industry

Paper has become an indispensable commodity in our day-to-day life. From cradle to grave, there are hardly any moment in our life when we can do without paper. In every field whether it is writing, reading, displaying, showing, codifying, monitoring, funding or even in industrial uses paper has come to stay a part of and parcel of our life style.

(i) *H.M.P. in KVI*—sector is one of the potential activity—which has tremendous scope for creating employment generation of women. We have in our various discussions confined our issues to basic Handmade paper making raw-materials, equipments, skill development and in a way not given serious stress to the diversification and value added HMP conversion items—which can double its employment generation avenue. We need also to have a marketing strategy—on clintele basis—the direction in which very serious holistic approach have not been initiated. When one opts for buying a UNICEF-calender or greeting cards (which are of Handmade Paper), it comes to one's mind automatically that the price we pay will go to assist a child. Similarly when one buyes a CRY-greeting card the feeling arises of supporting cause of a child. The *Handmade Paper* should boldly and loudly carry the message of save forest, protect environment—which is everybody's concern-all over the world. The opinion makers, media and market-awareness slogan in this direction needs to be initiated vigorously by KVIC to create a demand of eco-friendly Handmade Paper which also supports unemployed rural poor.

(ii) While we talk about handmade paper to a laymen it gives no message so as to what is mill made paper or handmade paper, like for Khadi-fabric at least the common man visualises a spinning wheel (*Charkha*)-to distinguish it from mill fabric, for handmade paper no such awareness or image bulding exercises have been evolved as part of publicity campaign. Here again a consumer (targeted) awareness campaign is necessary to convey the message that if there is a consumption of 1,00,000 greeting cards, 500 trees can be saved. This is responsibility of promotional agency bestowed with development of the industry.

(iii) There have not been any evaluation study of atleast HMP unit in the country to ascertain out of the category of the total HMP Product, what is the quantum of each category of end product such as writing, printing, stationary, decorative drawing or other types varieties of paper and their market value respectively. Perhaps HMP—may have edge/nitche of some specific category of paper in the market such as greeting, wedding, visiting, decorative, deckle—edge stationary, carry bags etc. Such a study/ survey is an immediate need of the industry which KVIC must immediately take-up encompassing its scope to exports market as well.

(iv) Input of various renewable energy—measures outlined in this paper particularly those which relate to drying of wet-paper must be taken up under Science and Technology project of KVIC and appropriate appliance and process know how so devised suitable to the industry need to be introduced. This would increase the impetus of industry as clean technology and effective environs friendly product.

(v) Successful handmade paper units, that have been able to tap export market, may be identified as growth unit of HMP and through them various nucleus may be created of extending their base for which adequate support and assistance may be provided to them for diversification and development of product, quality assurance and standardization facilities and assistance for giving training to persons whom they can provide sustainable employment.

Conclusion

Economic Development to be sustainable has to be "Eco and Environment Friendly". There is no simple rules or recipes to incorporate environmental dimension into process of development. However choices can be made, which eventually promote eco-friendly development even in rural sector projects. Understanding the eco-function identifying the issues involved and the options available are some of the key functions to protect conserve and improve environment and its bio-diversity on a sustainable basis. For a greater awareness on the various environmental issues, the best strategy (in rural areas) would be to link environmental protection with income generating activities for better involvement of rural poor and this is what HMP Industry stands for as a village industry conceived and promoted by Gandhiji. We all need to rededicate ourselves to the cause Gandhiji stood for, otherwise as Corre King (1995) said, " We may ignore Gandhiji at out own risk".

10

Scope of Renewable Energy in the Making of Handmade Paper

N.K. ROY

The outline of manufacturing process stated above reveals the nature of energy input required to be of two kinds, namely Mechanical and Heat Energy. One is required as Prime Mover to run the machines of Hollander beater, Calander, Hydraulic Press, Rag Chopper, Water Pumps etc. and the other for drying of handmade paper which is one of the serious bottle necks in rainy season.

Solar Energy Applications

India is in Sunny belt of the World. The country receives Solar Energy equivalent to more than 1000 trilion kWh per year, which is more than its total energy requirement. Though the energy density is low and availability is not continuous, it is now possible to harness this abundantly available energy very reliably for many purposes by converting its modular nature that can be appropriately used for applications. Few applications of the Renewable Solar Energy sources in Handmade Paper Industry could be as stated below:

Solar Water-Heating (SWH)

SWH system has been commercialised in many countries of the World including India. Its technical fesibility and economic viability has been established. It is now recognised as a reliable product that saves subtantial amount of electricity over other conventional fuels, leads to peak load reduction and prevents emissions of carbondioxid, a major green house gas. Depending upon the site, type of utilisation and the structure of electricity limit or fuel prices the pay-back period of the technology may vary from 2 to 6 years. To widespread use of the technology Ministry of Non-Conventional Energy Sources (MNES), Government of India, has been operating an inter subsidy scheme being implemented through Indian Renewable Energy Development Agency (IREDA) and a few designated Banks. This helps off-set initial cost of the system. Provides an acceptable pay-back period to various end-users, stimulates market and results in establishing a strong manufacturing base and after sales service network.

Application in HMP Industry: In all applications of pre-processing activities of raw material where heating, digestion, washing is required.

Solar-Heater

Solar dish, automatic tracked Parabolic Reflectors Standing outside the site of drying need-objects may reflect the Sun-Rays into the storage where wet-handmade paper sheets could be dried.

Solar-Air-Heating

Solar-Air-Heating technology can effectively be used for drying or curing of many varieties of HMP Products at their various stages of application including PED or full energy delivery (FED) unit. PED units require a back up energy system. Depending upon the drying process's required temperature, microclimatic and site conditions, the technology has the potential of saving considerable conventional energy in a variety of applications.

Various kinds of solar dryers have been developed and used in different field condition in the country. They include cabinet dryer based on solar wall-metal cladding technique, solar powered solar-air dryer based on solar hot water system coupled with liquid air-heat exchanger.

Solar-building

MNES, through expert agencies, have evolved designs and techniques to build Solar buildings, keeping in view the specifics need of the site/activity in areas of high altitudes, cold areas. The wet paper-drying Units of HMP industry can avail of the MNES facility/assistance for the purpose by making such Solar building exclusively for paper-drying, which is one of the major bottle neck of the industry.

Solar Photo Voltaic Programme

Solar photo voltaic (SPV) technology enables direct conversion of sunlight into electricity through semi-conductor devices called Solar Cells. Solar cells are inter connected and harmetically sealed to constitute a photo voltaic module. The photo voltaic module batteries, electronic etc. to constitute Solar photo voltaic (SPV) system and power plants. Photo voltaic system and power plants are highly reliable. Modulor in nature, cause no pollution and have long life. Such system and power plants have emerged as viable power sources for applications such as Lighting, Water Pumping, and Telecommunication and increasingly are used for meeting various kinds of Energy needs.

HMP units can augment energy needs by above SPV-system to save energy on one hand and make the HMP-product yet a step superior eco-friendly by adopting clean technology.

Bio-gas Energy

Bio-gas is produced using fermentation process wherein complex organic molecules present in organic waste are converted in Methane, Carbon-dioxide and traces of other gases. The gas is used for cooking and lighting purposes.

MNES—Government of India is implementing various programmes under the activity and provides financial and back-up support to harness this renewable energy.

The Bio-gas technology could be applicable for HMP units in following manners:

Dual Fuel Bio-gas Engines

Due to scarcity and shortages of Captive Electrical Power almost all HMP units are required to install generator sets of required capacity to sustain their activity. These generator-sets are run by diesel. Bio-gas and diesel mixed together can also be used to run these generators for which necessary dual-fuel gadgets have been developed and being run on bio-gas and are cost effective. The HMP units can explore establishment of required size of Bio-gas plants by themselves or tie-up with nearby Bio-gas plants owners for the purpose.

Bio-gas Power Project

Gaushalas, Dairy Firms, *Tabelas* are potential sources where large quantities of Cattle dungs etc. are available. HMP units can explore viability of formulating detailed project report for setting-up of Bio-gas project for which MNES—extends assistance in the form of preparing detailed project report (DPR). The quantum of assistance is upto Rs. 1.00 lakh per project of 100-250 kW and above 250 kW. Central subsidy at Rs. 20,000 per kW upto 25,000 kW.

Small Hydro Power Programme

The Small Hydro Power (SHP) *i.e.* 25 MW capacity is becoming a very viable option of power generations in selected areas where feasibility of establishment of such units exists. HMP units, located in such potential areas can benefit from MNES - support assistances in establishing SHP's have since been evaluated in almost all states, such as in Arunachal Pradesh—323, Maharashtra—234, U.P.—21, Uttaranchal—354, Tamil Nadu—147.

Energy from Waste

Waste generated from Urban and Industrial Sector increase continuously, some recent estimate have indicated that about 40 million tonnes of solid waste and 5000 million cubic meter of liquid waste is generated every year.

MNES has evolved patterns to support conversion of these waste to energy in stages of Waste to Power, Waste to Fuel, Fuel to Power and extends financial subsidy as per norms fixed from time-to-time.

Number of Bio-metharaties plants of industrial waste units have come in the country particularly in Sugar Mills, starch industry etc. HMP units can explore possibilities of tie-up/collaboration with similar industrial units, if they are situated nearby.

11

Scarcity of Raw Material for Handmade Paper Industry

A.K. SHARAN

In India varieties of paper are produced by Paper Mills as well as by Handmade Paper Industry. The main varieties produced by the mill sector are writing paper, tissue paper, kraft paper duplex board and speciality paper required in the Banking transactions. Similarly, the main varieties produced by the Handmade Paper Industry are drawing paper, cardsheets, file covers, fancy paper for gift pack, Bond Paper, Water Mark Paper for University Certificates etc.

As the 6.4 million tonne paper industry is expected to grow at the rate of 5.5 to 6 per cent annually and reaches 8 million tonnes by 2010, the acute problem of the supply of raw material will crop up. The demand of the paper/paper board will further increase with the overall economic growth, rising literacy levels and increasing penetration of books and periodicals in the country. Even after increase in demand of paper the per capita consumption has not increased substantially. The per capita consumption of paper and paper board in India is only 5 kg. as against 332 kg. in U.S.A. and the world average of 54 kg. The details of the data are given in Table 11.1.

Table 11.1: Paper Consumption Per Capita

S. No.	*Name of the Country*	*Consumption kg. yr/head*
1.	U.S.A.	332
2.	Sweden	247
3.	Japan	242
4.	The U.K.	206
5.	Korea	159
6.	China	29
7.	Thailand	32
8.	India	5
	World Average	**54**
	Asia Average	27

The need of the Handmade Paper is gaining importance not only for the general consumption but also because it tries to maintain ecological balance of the nature and saves deforestation. The production of Handmade Paper is 15,000 tonnes per annum which accounts for less then 0.5 per cent of current production of paper which is due to the scarcity of raw material, lack of R&D in the machinery and equipments, insufficient flow of fund to the sector, lack of demand of Handmade Paper and rarely available specialized institutes which provide Diploma/Certificate course in Handmade Paper Industry and of course taxation policy for the sector. My Paper is based on the scarcity of raw material.

The major problem Handmade Paper Industry is going to face in near future is the non-availability of hosiery cuttings and Cotton rags as it makes 80 per cent of the total raw material requirement of the Handmade Paper Industry. In winter season the availability of cotton hosiery cuttings decreases due to the manufacturing of woollen hosiery goods by the Hosiery Industry. Accordingly, the prices of the Hosiery cuttings also increases because of the short supply. It increases the Cost of Production of Handmade paper. Not only this, the output is also affected adeversely because natural drying of sheets also takes more time in winter season. The other reason is that the cotton Hosiery Cuttings as well as rags are again carded and converted into yarn for making various textile items. The situation is alarming.

The Handmade Paper Industry uses non-conventional raw material such as Waste Paper, Bagasse etc. (5%) in addition to Hosiery Cutting (80%) and rags (15%). In recent years it is noticed that the dependence of Paper Mills have increased using these raw materials specifically agro-waste. This is going to reduce the availability of Waste Paper and other Non-Conventional raw materials for the Handmade Paper Industry. It is therefore, suggested that government should intervene in the matter and large paper mills may be encouraged to use only wood pulp and other non-conventional raw materials may be kept reserved for the small paper mills and for Handmade Paper Industry. To manufacture one tonne of Paper/Paper Board, large mills require 2.8 tonnes of dry forest-based material which means 5 tonnes of palpable green wood maintaining approximately 25 to 30 per cent moisture. By a rough calculation 220 Eucalyptus trees or 460 bamboos are needed for the production of one tonne Paper/Paper Board.

If we have to solve the problem of raw material of Handmade Paper Industry we have to think over the same problems faced by Mill sector. The Indian Pulp and Paper Industry is really facing serious problem of supply of raw material which are predominantly forest-based fibres such as wood and bamboo. The fast depletion of these conventional raw material without simultaneous planned afforestation poses threat not only to this industry but to the entire eco-system causing concern to social scientists and environmentalists.

To meet the raw material requirement of the wood-based paper mills, plantations need to be developed on leased forest waste land. States of Andhra Pradesh, Karnataka and Chhattisgarh have already initiated steps in this regard and big Paper Mills are negotiating with these government for captive plantaions. At present, about 50 lakh tonnes of forest raw materials (bamboo and wood) are available. Small/Medium paper mills largely uses waste paper, wheat-straw, bagasse and rice straw whereas Handmade Paper Industry uses hosiery cutting, agro-waste, rags and waste paper. The availability of agro-based raw materials is estimated at more than 2.50 lakh tonnes per year in India. If straw and bagasse are used for the manufacture of paper it would amount to 50-60 lakh tonnes of paper.

To increase the availability of raw material to the Handmade Paper Industry a suitable policy may be developed on the same line as it is for the toilet soap in the village industry sector and sliver plants in the Khadi Sector. KVIC established its soap based plant and also encourages big institutions to establish soap base plants (Mother Unit) because every unit can't start these plants. Small units purchase soap base from such plants situated at Nasik, Churu, Akbarpur, Barabanki and other places and manufacture toilet soaps. Similarly, slivers are supplied to the Khadi Institutions from the sliver plants run by the KVIC. Mahasangh may establish the plant (Mother Pupling Unit) to make pulp from bagasse or wheat/rice straw and supply these raw materials to the needy Handmade Paper Units or it may encourage large Handmade Paper Units to establish such plants in the overall interest of all the units.

Efforts were made to utilize agro-fibres in Handmade Paper Sector with the pilot plant. Trials were conducted at Dehradun, Pune Wardha and few other places in the past. However, no systematic action has been taken to extend the results into the field in order to make use of agro fibre on sustainable basis.

Further, to discourage the large paper mills for using non-conventional raw material additional Excise Duty may be levied on them for using these type of raw materials. By this way it may be possible that more and more non-conventional raw material may be available for the Handmade Paper Industry. It may also reduce the cost of raw material for these units. In other way we can say that the cost of the material is related with the large and small paper mills. But it is a cause of great concern that the cost of raw material for the large paper mills are also a burning issue. In India the cost of raw material is three times more than in Indonesia. Consumption cost or raw material of various countries are given in Table 11.2 and the pulp furnish structure in percentage (India *vs.* World) are given in Table 11.3.

Table 11.2: Comparison of Cost of Raw Materials

S. No.	*Name of the Country*	*Cost of US$/Tonne*
1.	Indonesia	20
2.	Brazil	26
3.	Canada	31
4.	U.S.A.	36
5.	Australia	41
6.	India	60-75

Table 11.3: Pulp Furnish Structure in Percentage (India *vs.* World)

	Wood Pulp	*Non-wood*	*Waste Paper Pulp*
India	40	32	28
Pakistan	13	64	33
Bangladesh	34	16	50
China	15.3	42.3	42.4
World Average	**51**	**6**	**43**

Recommendations

1. Handmade Paper Industry may like initiative to establish mother pulping plant for manufacturing pulp from agro-waste.
2. Akhil Bhartiya Gramodhyog Mahasangh or All India Handmade Paper Association or any other NGO may start the project in Haryana or U.P. Later on other state federations may be encouraged to start such projects.
3. The cost of the project may be worked out by utilizing the services of experts in the field and the technology required to set up such Mother Units for Handmade Paper Industry.
4. Funds may be made available for the project under RISC programme of the KVIC on the same lines as

applicable for the North Eastern Region (i.e. 90% grant and 10% loan of the total cost of the project).

5. The project may be located in such states where sufficient quantity of agro-wastes are available.
6. The large Paper Mills may be encouraged to use wood pulp only.
7. Exemptions from all kinds of taxes may be provided to these types of Mother Pulping Plants which will cater to the needs of small Handmade Paper Units.

12

Bhimal Beol Fibre (*Grewia Oppsitifolia Roxb.*) for Handmade Paper Making

ATUL KUMAR and SAAKSHY AGARWAL

Introduction

Cotton rags and hosiery cuttings are the most preferred raw material for Handmade Industry having no ash and high alpha cellulosic content. This material produces paper with excellent strength properties.

However with increasing demand and production of handmade paper, the conventional raw materials may become scarce and costly. Industry would have to think for alternative raw materials which are locally available and easily pulpable. In this context KNHPI has been putting in concerted efforts to develop technology for pulping of such raw materials for handmade paper sector. Large number of raw materials have been evaluated by the Institute. Some of these like Banana, Jute, Sunn Hemp etc. have already found industrial use

Bhimal is a moderate sized tree of 45 ft. height and 4.5 ft. girth with a clear bole of 10-12 ft. It is widely grown in the Jammu, Himachal Pradesh and Uttaranchal *i.e.* Shiwalik hills. It has a short trunk and a spreading crown. It's wood is white having even and narrowly interlocked grains and fine texture. The bark yields a fibre length 1-1.5 mm used for cordage. It is also reported to be suitable for paper (Mathews, 345; Cross Bevan and King, Rep. Indian Fibres, 1887,9,39). The leaves and young twigs are much valued for fodder, especially in the hills.

Bhimal Beol fibre was received in the form of ropes from Himachal Pradesh Fibre Industry Federation, Una. The other local name of the fibres are *Biul, Biung, Behel,* etc. An attempt has been made to evaluate this raw material for different varieties of handmade papers. Laboratory as well as Pilot Plant studies were conducted. Results are reported in this paper. Through Sh. Laxmi Das Ex-Chairman KVIC, who is taking keen interest to develop a suitable alternative use for this abundantly grown tree.

Experimental

Table 12.1: Chemical Composition of Bhimal Fibre

Ash,%	4.0
Lignin,%	18.0
Cellulose,%	72.0

It was also found that the bast fibre has good amount of mucilagic content which can be utilized as a deflocculating agent during the paper making process.

Pulping

The raw material was converted into small size with the help of chopper to about 1.0 to 1.5 inches and was subjected to:

(i) Cold alkali digestion,
(ii) Hot alkali digestion, and
(iii) Alkaline Peroxide pulping.

Cold Digestion

The fibres of Bhimal were subjected to different chemical dosage under conditions of cold digestion as recorded in Table 12.2.

Table 12.2: Cold Alkali Digestion of Bhimal

S. No.	*Particulars*				
1.	Sodium hydroxide,%	4	6	8	10
2.	Time, hrs	24	24	24	24
3.	Temperature, °C	21	21	21	21
4.	Bath Ratio	1:10	1:10	1:10	1:10
5.	Pulp Yield, %	90.65	85.0	79.66	75.64
6.	Residual Active Alkali, gpl	0.65	1.06	1.86	2.04

After washing, the fibre was beaten in laboratory beater to 400 ml and 300 ml CSF. The beaten pulps were screened in vibratory screen before making laboratory sheets. The physical strength properties of the hand sheets are recorded in Table 12.3.

Table 12.3: Physical Strength Properties of Bhimal Pulp-Cold Digestion

S. No.	*Particulars*								
1.	NaOH %	4	4	6	6	8	8	10	10
2.	CSF, ml	400	300	400	300	400	300	400	300
3.	Tensile Index (Nm/gm)	24.1	26.2	28.51	49.70	50.1	55.06	60.0	69.06
4.	Tear Index (mN.m²/gm)	1.9	2.1	2.11	2.5	3.0	3.1	3.3	3.5
5.	Burst Index, (kPa.m²/gm)	1.5	1.7	1.96	2.00	2.5	2.85	3.1	3.14
6.	Folding Endurance (Double Fold)	140	152	453	637	800	917	1000	1023
7.	Brightness, %	43	43.1	43.30	43.9	44.2	44.9	45.0	45.2

Hot Alkali Digestion

The raw material was cooked with different dosages of sodium hydroxide at atmospheric pressure for three hours. Material to liquor ratio maintained at 1:8 in all the cases.

Table 12.4: Hot Alkali Digestion of Bhimal

S. No.	*Particulars*				
1.	Sodium hydroxide, %	4	6	8	10
2.	Yield, %	81.65	78.50	75.20	72.35
3.	Residual Active Alkali, gpl	nil	0.52	1.03	1.31

After washing, the fibre was beaten in laboratory beater to 400 ml and 300 ml CSF. The beaten pulp were screened in vibratory screen for making laboratory sheets. The physical strength properties of the hand sheets are recorded in Table 12.5.

Table 12.5: Physical Strength Properties of Bhimal Pulp-Hot Alkali Digestion

S. No.	*Particulars*								
1.	NaOH %	4	4	6	6	8	8	10	10
2.	CSF, ml	400	300	400	300	400	300	400	300
3.	Tensile Index (Nm/gm)	52.0	53	55	58.0	60	64.06	64.1	64.2
4.	Tear Index ($mN.m^2/gm$)	5.0	5.1	5.7	7.0	7.9	8.49	9.0	9.1
5.	Brust Index, ($kPa.m^2/gm$)	2.5	3.0	3.5	4.5	5.0	5.25	5.25	5.5
6.	Folding Endurance double Fold, %)	800	850	900	1000	1271	1319	1321	1330
7.	Brightness, %	39.8	39.9	40.1	40.2	40.6	41.0	41.1	41.2

Alkaline Peroxide Pulping Process

The raw material was cooked by Alkaline Peroxide Pulping Process with different dosages of sodium hydroxide and 2 per cent hydrogen peroxide after treating it with 0.5 per cent EDTA at pH-5.0. The time, temperature and bath ratio in all cases were maintained at 3 hrs, 95°C and 1:8 respectively.

Table 12.6: Alkaline Peroxide Pulping of Bhimal Beol

S. No.	Particulars				
1.	Sodium Hydroxide,%	4	6	8	10
2.	Hydrogen Peroxide,%	2	2	2	2
3.	PulpYield,%	79.98	75.64	71.25	68.54
4.	Residual Active Alkali, gpl	nil	0.15	0.96	1.52

After washing, the fibre was beaten in laboratory beater to 400 ml and 300 ml CSF. Laboratory hand sheets were made by screening the pulp in vibratory screen.The physical properties of the laboratory hand sheets are recorded in Table 12.7.

Table 12.7: Physical Strength Properties of Bhimal Pulp-Alkaline Peroxide Pulping

S. No.	Particulars								
1.	NaOH %	4	4	6	6	8	8	10	10
2.	CSF, ml	400	300	400	300	400	300	400	300
3.	Tensile Index (Nm/gm)	51.25	55.28	59.65	60.22	63.35	67.15	71.33	78.57
4.	Tear Index ($mN.m^2/gm$)	7.1	7.5	7.9	8.5	8.6	8.6	8.9	9.1
5.	Burst Index, ($kPa.m^2/gm$)	3.01	3.14	4.77	4.93	5.14	5.56	6.02	6.24
6.	Folding Endurance (Double Fold).	1054	1528	2996	3103	4585	4965	5145	5336
7.	Brightness, %	41.5	42.35	46.5	47.4	50.6	51.2	53.35	54.6

Table 12.8: Comparison of Bhimal, Banana and Jute Pulps (APP-8%NaOH, 2% H_2O_2)

S. No.	Particulars	*Bhimal*	*Banana*	*Jute*
1.	CSF ml.	300	300	300
2.	Tensile Index(Nm/gm)	67.15	77.44	68.9
3.	Tear Index(mN^2/gm)	8.60	19.91	7.10
4.	Brust Index ($kPa.m^2/gm$)	5.56	8.62	5.10
5.	Folding Endurance (Double Fold)	4965	5000	2347
6.	Brightness, %	51.20	48	21.01

Result and Discussion

Proximate chemical analysis of Bhimal bast recorded in Table 12.1 shows that it is characterized by high cellulosic content and low lignin content, which makes it suitable for consideration for utilizations for handmade paper making.

Result of pulping by cold soda process recorded in Table 12.3 indicate that pulps in yields varying from 75.64 to 91 per cent could be obtained with varying chemical dosages. The pulps possess moderate strength properties. However better results were obtained in the case of hot soda pulping (Tables 12.4 and 12.5). Optimum results with respect to pulp yield and strength characteristic were obtained by pulping the raw material with 8 per cent hot caustic. Residual alkali is about 1.03 gpl, which will have to be taken care of when considering this process for industrial application.

Results of Alkaline Peroxide Pulping are recorded in Table 12.6. Pulps in yields varying from 72 per cent to 82 per cent could be produced from this fibre. A perusal of strength characteristic of the pulp recorded in Table 12.7 reveals that pulps of very good strength characteristics could be produced by pulping this raw material by alkaline peroxide process. Strength characteristics of APP pulps are much superior to hot and cold soda pulps.

A comparison of strength characteristic of Bhimal pulp with those of Banana and Jute fibres by cooking with 8 per cent alkali and 2 per cent peroxide are recorded in Table 12.8. The results indicate that Bhimal pulp produced under similar conditions gives pulp having better brightness compared to Banana and Jute pulps. Although tensile, tear and burst in case of Bhimal are lower than Banana, but these are comparable to Jute Pulp. The results show that Bhimal is a suitable raw material for producing variety of handmade papers which is supported by the Pilot Plant trials.

REFERENCES

"Forest Flora of the Chakrata, Dehradun and Saharanpur forest division Uttar Pradesh" being a revised and enlarged edition of "The forest flora of the Siwalik and Jaunsar forest divisions, U.P." by Upendranath Kanjilal, Rai Bahadur, F.L.S Extra Deputy Conservator of Forests.

The Wealth of India, Volume IV.

13

Value Addition—Quality Aspects

D.S.R. RAJU

Today, after reaching great heights in global market as one of the leading eco-friendly paper, handmade paper market now demands creative and economic value addition.

Value addition, in general is a very crucial factor. It has to be highly creative, economical, production oriented. Before planning any value addition, we must keep in two major factors in mind. First the market demand and secondly the life cycle of the value addition. Market demand forecast is important because of regular change of colours and patterns. This will change from region to region, for example: U.S. market is different than the European and gulf market. It is advisable to plan in such a way that the value addition is universally accepted. For the life cycle, we must have an idea how much time this can be in the market. It may be more useful if one can plan value addition in phases instead of all at one go. This will help to see change in the pattern and stay in the market for a longer time with minimum efforts.

Our market is totally unorganized. We do not have any regular and fair interactions with the global player, no one can be blamed for this. *This is mainly due to the lack of trust and misunderstanding.* Also in creativity once the idea clicks, many people can copy the concept very easily. Ours is a very basic and traditional art based market and to come up with more creative/newer varieties we do not require any science/ technology. What is needed is a sense of style and acceptability. These days more energy is spent copying the creativity of others. But this is the market trend and we have to live with this phenomena. Now if we analyze the quality factors from a close angle, there are two major raw materials in the product making (1) Hardboard (gatta), (2) Adhesives (glues).

Hardboards: Hardboard is available in various qualities. First let us understand how a gatta is manufactured. Gatta is manufactured right from filthiest raw materials like road garbage to good paper waste and pulp waste. So depending on the quality of raw material, the strength of the board depends. Who ever does what ever, if one has to survive in the market in the present scenario, one should and one must follows the basic quality requirements. Handmade paper carries more of a fabric properties then the normal paper made from the pulp. Hardboard is the skeleton of the product, if compromised on the quality, the product will be defective. If analysed on the financial front, the price hike will be adjusted. Normally what happens is while sampling we normally use good raw materials. But while placing an order the customer starts bargaining, many times they will opt for a cheaper supplier. Also, the quality of paper at the time of sampling is different than the paper quality at final production. This also plays a major role while converting.

Conversion Experience

The converter is the sole responsible person for all the good and bads. It is advisable to have a sample of the final lot to be approved. Time is also a crucial factor and we always work under tight schedules. But to save last hour complication, it is better to have proper scheduling an necessary approval. The approval may definitely delay the production by few hours but solve the last moment embarrassment. To accommodate the cost variation we always try to cut down cost on gatta, primarily. Good quality of gatta takes less time in drying than the cheaper quality. The major problem with cheaper quality gatta is de-shaping. Once the gatta gets de-shaped, it never comes back to original form. As we said earlier, handmade paper carries more of fabric properties, basically we are disintegrating the fabric and again reintegrating it. So when we apply the glues, the paper expands slightly and when dried, this will shrink, this causes deformity or de-shaping of the product. We must understand the strength of paper first. There is no conventional method to measure it, the best way to know is to make few samples, and dry them open without any pressure on some and few under pressure. Drying time has to be at least 12 hours in normal weather conditions and 24 hours in winters. The drying time taken is more for cheaper quality. The adhesives choosen plays a major role, water base adhesives will take longer than synthetic adhesives. But this is essential rather compulsory to save the last moment embarrassments. We have no control over the gatta and we cannot check each and every gatta, we blindly go by the sticker (*chepi*) on it. There is lot of duplicacy in gatta also. So better to check the end results before the mass production begins. The easiest solution is to make production samples.

Surface of gatta also plays a major role. To get the best quality results it is wise to use MDF/LDF board;. 2 mm thickness board is equivalent to 40 ounce gatta. MDF boards are light in weight, better strength and smooth external surfaces. These Boards can be used with gatta also. Cost difference between the gatta and MDF board is almost double. For customer, MDF board will work out cheaper, because of the quality, finishing and weight. This should be explained to the client how the difference of price will be compensated/saved in their freight rates. So it is strongly recommended to use MDF Boards. But MDF Boards have their own drawbacks, mainly cutting. They are not compatible with paper dye cutting/normal cutting machines. They can be cut in size and any shape by saw (wood/board) cutting machine, each and every piece has to be cut individually. This is again an additional cost factor. To get similarity between all pieces (to get high accuracy) it is advisable to print the stencil marks on the boards, so that all cutting worker will follow the same cutting line. We can use both gatta and MDF board together. Straight cutting is easy with the board so we can use the gatta on front (like in photo frames) and board on the back. We can use both water based and synthetic adhesives with board. Lastly the surface of the gatta is not very smooth, to get better finish normally we use 150 gsm paper, but in case of boards, we can use even 60-70gsm paper, to get smooth surface (we personally screen printed MDZF boards in six colours).

Adhesives: Use of adhesives are equally tricky. The type of adhesives to be used will purely depend on ones own judgment. Use of adhesives vary from paper to paper. For some paper (especially dark colours) we can't use synthetic adhesives as they change the colour (some times black spot will appear) basically due to chemical reaction. But when we use water-based adhesives (normally *lye*), there are chances of fungus in the products, if the products were not upper surface only, but it means 100 per cent moisture free from outside as well as inside. Normally once we complete one side we immediately start pasting the paper on the other side. This is a wrong practice. The moisture gets sandwiched in between the papers. This is the main cause for foul smell and fungus. There has to be at least 12-24 hours gap between the two, this basically depends on the quality of gatta. If MDF board with the synthetic adhesives (fevicol) is used, then even 2-3 hours are more than sufficient. In home made *lye* people normally use copper sulphate (*nelathotha*) to make the *lye* bonding stronger. But, firstly *nelathotha* leaves stain on the paper and secondly it chemically reacts with the paper colours. These day's better readymade *lyes* are available at economical rates in bulk packings. But use of synthetic adhesives will increase strength of the product, dries faster and chances of fungal is minimum. Quality will pay you in the long run. Just to save few rupees, we are loosing few lac of rupees as well as the credibility of Indian Handmade paper products. Please forget "chaltahai" and in Handicrafts small deviation is acceptable but not deterioration of quality. Just by changing our mindset and becoming quality conscious we can do wonders.

We welcome your ideas, suggestions, opinions and your criticism on this topic, to improve ourselve while educating fellow artisans, on my e-mail address greeengallery@yahoo.com.

14

Handmade Paper Industry Growing Opportunities

VIJAY KUMAR

Introduction

Indian Handmade Paper Industry has a long history and has traversed a formidable path of success, and today has become an attractive industry for both investment and profitability. In olden times, much before independence the handmade paper produced by small number of traditional paper makers known as *'kagzis'* was of a simple variety used predominantly by the provincial courts for their records and also by universities/ institutions for Degrees/Certificates. Today the Indian Handmade Paper Industry, together with the creative value addition by the converters, artisans and designers produces handmade papers which are sought after by the manufacturers, whole sellers/retailers and society all over the world for various applications, viz., invitations, gifts, writing, printing and many other uses. Our papers have earned awards or are selected for display in the latest 'Trends Pavilions' of major reputed trade fairs like the PAPERWORLD in Frankfurt, Germany every year.

In addition, the Indian handmade paper is truly Eco-friendly in nature as it is made from 100 per cent cotton rags and no wood pulp is used. Even if waste paper is mixed with cotton rags to produce a low grade/low cost paper the product still retains its Eco-friendly characteristic. The Indian handmade paper as decorative papers can be sold or used for various applications in the coming years.

Review of Development Till 2000

As already stated earlier the handmade paper was initially made only for limited applications, *i.e.*, for court records, degrees/ certificates awarded by the institutions etc. These had the archival characteristics (acid free) wherein animal glue sizing was applied externally. Gradually, flower petals, straw, grass and silk fibres, colours were added to the pulp to produce decorative papers for domestic use. However, these papers had limited applications till almost 1990 when the Western World caught its fancy and started using the papers widely for Gifts and Wrappings etc.

The production was confined to clusters of traditional handmade paper makers called the *'kagzis'* settled in various parts of India. However, after 1960 with the support of the Khadi and Village Industries Commission (KVIC), many other people took to handmade paper making. In the year 1994, there were approximately 400 handmade paper units spread all over India, and most of these (about 70%) were concentrated in Northern and Western India.

Unfortunately till 1990 there was no major investment made by either the Government or by the private sector towards improvement of technology in the handmade paper industry. With the coming up of the new generation looking for opportunities for growth in unconventional sectors such as handmade paper industry together with the availability of support in the form of training and financial assistance both from Banks and the KVIC, many small handmade paper units were established and commenced production of handmade papers/value addition. In order to cope with the increased demand of handmade papers, both in the domestic market and abroad, Cylinder Mould Machines using the same cotton rag pulp, as used for making the handmade papers by conventional lifting method, were gradually introduced in the private sector. After considerable pressure from the industry, the cylinder mould technique was approved and recognized by the KVIC.

A significant milestone in the development of handmade paper industry was achieved in 1990 with the establishment of Kumarappa National Handmade Paper Institute near Sanganer, Jaipur as a United Nations Development Programme (UNDP) project and assisted by the KVIC. This institute was formally inaugurated in 1997 as an autonomous body and is doing a commendable work towards imparting training to young entrepreneurs as well as unertaking some research and development projects which will be useful to the handmade paper industry.

All India Handmade Paper Industries Association, has also made singnificant contribution towards the development of the handmade paper industry by bringing together a large number of producers, converters and traders including exporters etc. connected with the handmade paper industry on one common platform and organizing seminars and publication of Souvenirs on Handmade Paper Industry. These souvenirs published every two years serve as a useful directory of the Handmade Paper Manufacturers, Traders Manchinery Manufacturers and Institutions connected with the Handmade Paper Industry. In December 1995, a Seminar on 'Handmade Paper—Emerging Global Opportunities' organized jointly by the All India Handmade Paper Industries Association, KVIC and UNDP drew a big response from young entrepreneurs not only form all over India but also from neighbouring SAARC countries.

By rough estimates, by the year 2000 there were 1000 handmade paper units spread out all over India. An equal number of entrepreneurs were engaged either in value addition or trading in handmade paper. Together, they contributed to approximately Rs. 100 crores worth of domestic as well as export sales. Thus, the period between 1990 and 2000 was the most significant in the development of handmade paper industry, which can be termed as the period of 'Handmade Paper Revolution.'

Limitations and Alternatives

While the period between 1990 and 2000 can be termed as a 'Handmade Paper Revolution' during which a commendable development and growth was achieved, there is still a lot to be done if the handmade paper industry is to continue and maintain its pace of development. Some of the areas, which were observed and needed attention during the above period, are discussed in the succeeding paragraphs alongwith suitable alternatives.

Technology

The technology that is used in the handmade paper industry is an old, though well proven technology. There is however, need for technology upgradation by introducing innovation, making the machines like the 'Hollander Beater' more energy efficient. Use of cylinder mould machines though assist in increase in production, these are at the cost of reducing the employment opportunities which are more with the conventional paper making method. Use of low cost and efficient paper driers are absolutely necessary for increasing paper production during the monsoon/rainy or the winter season by speeding up the paper drying. Kumarappa National Handmade Paper Institute can play a vital role in this aspect.

Raw Material

There is always a shortage of the availability of cotton rags or if available the cost is very high. The much talk about use of alternate raw materials to replace the expensive cotton rags has not made any progress to be able to offer a viable on a commercial scale. The answer, probably, lies in allowing import of cotton pulp in large quantities without any or at a low rate of import duty so that the raw material essentially required for production of handmade papers is easily available and at a lower cost.

While some manufacturing units might already be resorting to partly mixing waste papers with the cotton rags there is a need to study the technical implications of this alternative and recommend a suitable technique so that handmade papers could be produced to the desired specifications at a lower cost.

Another major problem that is being experienced by almost all the handmade paper manufacturing units is the presence of synthetic fibres in the cotton rags which can not be dyed in any colour and show up as white spots in a coloured paper leading to its rejection. If a suitable alternative could be found for this synthetic fibres then it will reduce a lot of rejection and also make the low cost cotton rags suitable for production. Efforts need to be made to find an early solution to this problem.

Packaging

Packaging of handmade papers does not as much attention as its production. Most of the manufacturers believe that their responsibility is over once they have packed and dispatched the handmade paper to the buyer. As a result the buyer receives the handmade papers with bent corners, in dirty or partly wet conditions unsuitable for sale or intended use. Most of the transport companies in India do not take enough care to avoid damage to the handmade papers during transportation.

Many buyers abroad have complained that they received the papers or products in damaged condition and are unable to sell these. This results in a considerable loss to buyer and the exporter besides the loss of reputation.

Packaging has a very important impact on marketing. Good packaging is essential so that it not only protects the papers or the products during handling and transportation but is also attractive and made from environment friendly materials. Many countries have restrictions for use of polythene bags and wood as outer packing material.

Environmental Factors

Availability and Conservation of Water

The handmade paper making process requires considerable use of water. Majority of the manufacturing units depend on the ground water sources which are fast getting depleted and need to be conserved for more important uses like domestic consumption as well as for agricuture. In fact during the next decade and after, availability of water is going to be a major factor, which will govern the production of handmade paper.

There is, thus, a dire need for installation of a suitable water recycling in every manufacturing unit. The system should be developed by Kumarappa National Handmade Paper Institute or any other agency under its guidance or supervision.

Ground Water Pollution

As water is an important resource for both the human sustenance as well as production of handmade paper, it is essential that the ground water resources should not get polluted due to the discharge of the effluents from the manufacturing units. In spite of claims that the handmade paper industry is a non-polluting industry, there is a need to study and really determine the extent of pollution being caused as result of discharge of these effluents, though it might not contain chemicals, yet these can cause considerable harm over long-term as these contain amounts of bleach and colour dye residues.

Use of Solar, Wind and Bio Energy

Use of Solar Energy, Wind Energy or Bio Gas to operate the machinery and for lighting will be useful in reducing the overall costs besides promoting use of the natural sources of energy.

Marketing of Handmade Paper and Products

The handmade paper which once used to be made in the form of simple plain paper or mottled with flower petals, or fibres like straw or silk etc. has undergone a great change during the period of 'Handmade Paper Revolution' and is available today in many colours, textures and with value additions beyond one can imagine. All these are a result of creative trends which have resulted in making the Indian handmade papers as most attractive and sought after papers by customers both in India and abroad.

Marketing of Handmade Paper is similar to the Fashion *i.e.*, Garments, Gifts and Accessories. There is a constant change in style, colours which might vary from one country to another and from one season to another. Many new manufacturing units are aware about the latest trends and start producing according to their own imagination. These units then try to sell their products. This invariably leads to frustration as the papers do not sell. The *'mantra'* for successful marketing of handmade papers or for that matter any product is *'Make What Sells'*. This is better said than done, and will require a good knowledge about the latest trends in the domestic as well as the export market. It comes by lot of hard work being quality conscious, market survey, visits to foreign trade fairs research from websites, hiring of designers to create new designs etc. Also please remember that what sells in the domestic market might not be successful for export. Success *will come naturally if one is more creative and has the ability to find or anticipate the market moods (likes and dislikes).*

To facilitate the handmade paper manufacturers to understand and learn about the latest trends in the fashion/ accessories market, it is recommended that capsule courses be organized in association with Institute of Fashion Technology, New Delhi.

By 2010 the market for handmade papers and products, both in the domestic as well as the export market is expected to grow by at least ten times from the current levels. However, this growing potential can only be tapped with creativity and keeping abreast with the market requirements.

Conclusion

In the coming years handmade papers and products will continue to dominate their leading position in the world market as the most attractive decorative papers. This will however be only possible if we continue to create innovative and attractive designs, textures and value addition. Making papers in small quantities according to customer's requirements of colours and textures is the greatest strength of this industry. In spite of country in the coming years, this industry will continue to be a labour intensive industry creating job opportunities to a large number of rural or semi-rural men and women. At the same time the handmade paper industry provides a good opportunity for investment and growth for those who are sincere and creative in their efforts.

15

Hemp: Environment and Society

M. SADIQUE

For the last couple of decades, environmental awareness is growing at a galloping rate throughout the world but unfortunately without any professional approach. Preservation of environment is of course should be the top priority but not at the cost of development and growth of society. Rather we must adhere to the sustainable development and while taking initiatives for the development, simultaneous efforts should be made to protect the environment by adopting appropriate technological processes, which take due care of environment. Environmental policies in India so far remained directionless without holistic approach and had objectives to achieve any political goals. The impending global crisis posed by increasing environmental degradation and ecological imbalance has created deep concern for the conservation and proper care of the biosphere in which we live. A healthy environment leads to a healthy society whether its Urban or Rural.

The environmental management of Rural India is still worst. Because despite various drawbacks in the environmental policies the environment of Urban areas is preserved to a great extent but Rural areas are far away from the environmental policies. In fact agricultural operation causes some of the rural environmental crisis but degradation of environment also affects agriculture. Depending upon the nature of soils and agriculture environment of a particular region selection of appropriate crops may also help conserve the environment as well as develop the living style of the rural society.

The areas between the Kumaon and Garhwal hills are known to be the best for the crops of hemp, particularly the areas which have been cleared very recently. Apart from this the districts of Almora and Nainital, parts of Punjab, Bihar, and West Bengal also provide suitable environment for cultivation of hemp. The potential of this crop is not yet known to the extent it can help in the development of environment both Social and Physical. Hemp can also play a vital role in the development of rural areas where it can be cultivated though it is commonly known in India as a source of narcotics like *ganja, siddhi* and *charas.* It is also used in the manufacture of tissue paper. Since the hemp plant is a source of three narcotics *e.g. siddhi* from leaves, *charas* from its gum and *ganja* from its floral axis; it is called Trimurti in Sanskrit. In some parts of India it is also used for religious purposes like while celebrating Shivaratri and Durga Puja.

In European countries, parts of China, Japan and U.S.A. due regard is given to the fibre value of hemp and it is principally grown for its valuable fibre contents. The hemp plant requires a moderately rich, friable, well drained sandy loam for its growth when extraction of fibre is the main aim. Depending upon different climatic and natural conditions a number of varieties of hemp fibre have been developed. Methods of fibre extraction also vary from the country. The yield of fibre normally ranges from 100 to 600 kg. an acre. However it is found to be 800 kg. if suitable environment is available and appropriate care is taken. There are two kinds of hemp found in India. One is called Khurbanga or *Jungli Bhang.* It grows wild throughout the sub-Himalayan regions in all situations attaining a considerable height during rainy seasons. However this plant is of not viable. The recovery from it does not remunerate even the poorest class for the trouble bestowed on it. Nor does it contain fibre of the class that can be put to some use.

Since this plant gives better fibre at high altitude places, it may will be tried in hill states of North Eastern India and this fibre can be used for weaving shawls and garments in loins loom used extensively in those areas.

The fibre blended with wool or acrylic fibre can be used for poducing knit wear for the areas where cold is moderate.

Hemp for Medicines

Apart from the use of hemp plant for extraction of fibre it has got tremendous potential for use as a medicinal substance. It has got properties of intoxicant, sedative, narcotic, antispasmodic, analgesic and stigmatic. *Siddhi,* which is prepared from the leaves of the hemp plant, itself is considered as medicinal as it is sedative, intoxicant, cause sleepiness, analgesic and good urinator.

It is applied in respect of nervous diseases, hydrophobia, delirium, alcoholism, hay fever, gonorrhea various skin diseases etc. It is also effective in case of excessive menstrual flow, bleeding of uterus, delayed child birth and for shrinkage and expansion of uterus. In some opinions it causes anemia, indigestion, impotency and swelling of the body. Snuff of dry leaves clears the brain and the extract if applied externally cures dandruff and skin diseases. Few drops of extract as ear drop relieves earache.

Ganja is prepared from the matured flowers and considered medicinal with milk if applied externally stops bleeding from the bleeding piles. It is also applied externally in case of gonorrhea. Those who smoke *ganja* for a long period die of lungs or swelling of the body.

The seed yields 30 to 35 per cent fatty oil. It is a soft oil with higher unsaturation. It is normally used for paint and varnish industry but can also be used as massage oil and soluble herbs.

Lastly one very interesting information to mention here that the white rope which is tied to the National Flag of India for its unfurling has been specified under BIS code to be of hemp fibre.

The other one is the real hemp which is a cultivated variety and grown chiefly on high lands in the well prepared and abundantly manured soils close to village or on recently cleared lands by baring primeval forests, the soil being rich to ensure a superior growth of the plant and abundant crop without any manure for one season. The best production comes from elevation of 1500 to 2500 metres above sea level. For the purpose of recovering the fibre the stalks are then soaked in water for about 15 days in tanks or slowly flowing streams, and beaten with mallets to give a superior fibre. It is then dried in the sun, striped off and again beaten for a yield of soft fibre.

Hemp for Fibre

Hemp fibre is strong, lustrous and durable. When carefully prepared it has a light colour. Its principal use is for twine, fine cordage, fabrics—chiefly canvas or tarpaulins, sail cloth and sacking. In America it is used in the manufacture of sponges. It is also used for caulking boats, pumps, engines and other machinery. In India it is used to a limited extent for manufacture of sacks of synthetic fibres.

Considering quality and the properties of this fibre there is certainly great scope to expand its use and scope for greater value addition. Light in colour, good in lustre, spinnable quality and quality to accept dies are some to the properties which can be exploited for utilising the fibre for production of garments. However it should also to be noted that this fibre can not be spun to a very high count like jute or cotton. But in bulk of garments industry the coarser fibre can also be used for winter garments. This thought is now under circulation after bulk of population is discarding synthetic fibres and switching over to eco-friendly fibre.

As population is growing higher and higher with shortage of supply, conventional material like cotton, silk woollen, linen etc., there is a search for alternate fibre and to some extent hemp fibre fits in. Some attempts are being made but limited to certain fashion garments in certain pockets.

Conclusion

The cultivation of hemp therefore has great potential not only to give us fashion garments and variety of medicines but also it can ensure large employment opportunities in the rural sector. This will help poverty alleviation, healthy society and an healthy environment.

The cultivation of this crop for medicinal purposes will definitely create employment opportunities for the educated unemployed youth by way of establishment of processing units for the medicines out of the different parts of the hemp plant.

It is therefore required to establish research centres to work further on hemp because at present the only research being carried out on this plant is related either with narcotics or its medicinal virtues.

An appropriate plan is therefore needed for research, development of prototype pilot projects, extension, education and training on hemp fibre to explore the possibilities of new types of garments with new fashion yet eco-friendly.

16

Improved Process for Conversion of Shredded Currency Waste into Different Varieties of Handmade Papers

R.K. JAIN, A.K. SHARMA, BALESHWER PRASAD, ATUL KUMAR, MOHD. ESA KHAN and SAAKSHY AGARWAL

Introduction

The effective disposal of shredded currency waste has been one of the major challenges before Reserve Bank of India. There are nearly 19 branches of Reserve Bank of India, located in the metro and other big cities of India that are generating significant quantities of shredded currency paper waste in the form of compressed briquettes.

As per estimates, nearly 10,000 T/annum of shredded currency in the form of briquettes is available which has not been effectively utilized, thereby creating problems of solid waste disposal.

The earlier method of disposal of shredded currency waste was a tedious task wherein the punched notes and bits had to be bunt within R.B.I. premises under the supervision of team of senior officials of Reserve Bank of India. In this process, the torned notes used to be destroyed by incineration and had been the most costly discard management option producing toxic ash.

The process of burning the currency notes was causing the problem of air pollution since the currency notes coated with chemicals, pigments and colours release toxic gaseous and harmful pollutants. This method of disposal was not only non-eco-friendly and also caused lot of concerns for global warming.

Subsequently, at the intervention of pollution control authorities, the currency waste paper was shredded to 1/10th mm size to convert into the briquettes employing the briquetting plant imported from Germany, which used a very high pressure to convert shredded currency waste into briquettes. In one of its endeavour of Reserve Bank of India to utilize this valuable shredded currency paper waste which basically is manufactured from high quality fibrous raw material like cotton and hemp, Kumarappa National Handmade Paper Institute could develop one of the promising technology for converting shredded currency waste into handmade paper and paper board which finds potential application after its conversion into file covers, letter pads, pamphlets and other stationery items. The Kumarappa National Handmade Paper Institute is the only one of its kind in Asia to develop this technology which has been patented in the past for making handmade paper and paper boards and converting paper board to produce file covers which are supplied back to Reserve Bank of India and some of the government officials like Khadi and Village Commission etc.

As a part of its Research and Development activities, the Institute has been continuously trying to improve the process to make it simple, less capital intensive and to produce the paper and paperboard useful for making handmade paper products in cost effective way.

Raw Material

The currency notes are produced from good quality cellulosic raw material like cotton and hemp in addition to chemicals like resins. The cellulosic raw material employed in making currency notes have good strength properties because of the morphological nature of fibre with good fibre length. The physico-chemical analysis of shredded currency waste was carried out for various parameters of interest before converting material into paper. The results of the analysis are shown in Table 16.1.

The data shown in Table 16.1 indicated that the shredded currency waste could be better source of cellulosic raw material containing higher quantities of alpha cellulosic with negligible quantities of lignin therefore it has been possible to convert it into pulp with minimum requirement of pulping chemicals. The higher quantities of ash and other tacky materials, inks, pigment in shredded currency waste paper may require specific treatment conditions which were optimized at Kumarappa National Handmade Paper Institute for converting it into the handmade paper useful for various paper products.

Table 16.1: Proximate Analysis of Shredded Currency Waste Paper

S. No.	*Particulars*	*Result*
1.	Cold water solubility, %	5.0
2.	Hot water sulubility, %	12.5
3.	1 N NaOH solubility, %	18.5
4.	Alocohol-benzene solubility, %	6.0
5	Holocellulose, %	88.32
6.	α-Cellulose, %	83.66
7.	Klasson Lignin, %	1.2
8.	Ash, %	3.70

Earlier Process Developed at KNHPI for Conversion of Shredded Currency Waste into Handmade Paper

Having set up a briquetting plant imported from Germany to convert the shredded currency waste into solid briquettes of size 15 cm × 8.75 cm × 6 cm, Reserve Bank of India is still facing the problem of storage of huge heaps of briquettes and did not find an effective way to utilize and disposal of briquettes in an economical way. Subsequently Reserve Bank of India approached Kumarappa National Handmade Paper Institute to explore the potential of converting the waste material into handmade paper/handmade paper products. Having done extensive Research and Development work, Kumarappa National Handmade Paper Institute could develop a technology for conversion of the shredded currency waste into a good quality handmade paper during the year 2000 for which a patent was also filed by KNHPI. After successful laboratory scale studies, the process was up-scaled to pilot scale using the support of Reserve Bank of India to integrate the existed facilities with some more equipments for effective processing of the shredded currency waste into handmade paper.

The handmade paper and paper board produced at pilot scale of Kumarappa National Handmade Paper Institute was converted into various paper products like file covers, envelopes, pamphlets and other stationary items which were supplied continuously to various branches of Reserve Bank of India and KVIC offices.

Details of the process conditions for converting the shredded currency waste into handmade paper is shown in Table 16.2.

Table 16.2: Process Conditions of the Earlier Process for Recycling Shredded Currency Waste into Handmade Paper

S. No.	*Particulars*	*Improved Process*
1.	**Pulping conditions**	
	Sodium hydroxide	4%
	EDTA	0.50%
	Sodium Silicate	1.0%
	Hydrogen Peroxide	2.0%
	Bath Ratio	1:4
	Temperature	120°C
	Time	4 hours
2.	**Hydrapulping /Beating/Refining characteristics**	
	Hydrapulping time, hrs.	1.0
	Follow by	
	Beating time, hrs.	1.0
	CSF, ml	300
	Power consumption in hydrapulping, kWh/kg.	0.175
	Followed by	
	Power consumption in Beater, kWh/kg.	0.175
	Total power consumption in mechanical action	***kWh/kg.***
3.	Cost of paper/paper board produced (Rs. kg.)	Rs. 11-12.350

The raw material was cooked in rotary digestor and the cooked raw material was dumped for further processing.

Washing and Sheet Making

The cooked pulp is washed in the potcher washer with the help of a rotating drum washer provided with a wire mesh and sent to beater followed by Cylinder Mould Vat Machine for sheet making. The process is shown in Fig. 16.1.

Improved Process for Converting Shredded Currency Waste into Handmade Paper

In view of the opening up of the economy and stiff competition both in domestic and global market, there is a need to continuously improvise the process and products in a cost effective manner while improving its quality.

With this objective, the efforts were continued to improvise the process for recycling of the shredded currency waste to convert into handmade paper. This was aimed to improve the techno-economic viability and to make the process simple and less capital intensive so that the cost of the paper produced could be further reduced. Having done the extensive research at Kumarappa National Handmade Paper Institute, it was observed that there is a possibility to improve the process by elimination of certain chemicals and also making certain process modifications during mechanical treatment of cooked fibre.

In the recent improved process, use of EDTA, sodium silicate, hydrogen peroxide has been eliminated and instead of using hydrapulper/beating, the cooked material is directly taken for beating and/or refining to provide mechanical action.

The process conditions of the improved process for converting shredded currency into handmade paper is as given in Table 16.3 and flow chart is given as Fig. 16.1.

As in the earlier process, the raw material was cooked in a rotary digestor and the cooked raw material was dumped for further processing. The cooked pulp is washed in the

Potcher washer with the help of a rotating drum washer provide with a wire mesh and mechanically treated by passing it through refiner instead of hydrapulper as in the earlier process wherein the time could be reduced from two hours (one hour in hydrapulper followed by one hour in beater) to only half an hour in the improved process used in refining. The remaining process 75 per cent reduction in energy has been achieved using refiner and if refiner is not available still there is a possibility of saving of nearly 60 per cent energy even with the use of beater.

Table 16.3: Process Conditions of Improved Process for Recycling Shredded Currency Waste into Handmade Paper

S. No.	*Particulars*	*Improved Process*
1.	**Pulping conditions**	
	Sodium hydroxide	4%
	Bath Ratio	1:4
	Temperature	120°C
	Time	3 hours
2.	**Beating/Refining characteristics**	
	Beating time, hrs.	¾
	or	
	Refining time, hrs.	½
	CSF, ml.	300
	Power consumption in beater, kWh/kg.	0.131
	or	or
	Power consumption in refiner, kWh/kg.	0.087
3	Cost of handmade paper board, Rs./kg.	Rs. 9-10

Results and Discussions

Comparison of strength properties of handmade paper produced from shredded currency waste employing two different processes.

The strength properties of the sheets made in pilot plant of the Institute was tested for physical properties. The results of the same are given in Table 16.4 and shown in Fig. 16.1.

From the results shown in Tables 16.2, 16.3 and 16.4, it is evident that:

1. Elimination of certain chemicals used during cooking like EDTA, Hydrogen Peroxide and Sodium Silicate in the improved process did not have any adverse effect on the process.
2. Power consumption and time of mechanical treatment was considerably reduced wherein energy consumption was reduced from 0.35 kWh/kg. of pulp to 0.13 kWh/kg. of pulp indicating 60 per cent reduction in energy and time was also reduced considerably.
3. Without compromising the brightness of pulp, strength properties of the pulp produced in the improved process significantly improved wherein Tensile Index, Tear Index and Burst Index improved by 10 per cent, 30 per cent and 10 per cent respectively where double fold was improved by 1.5 to 2 times.

Table 16.4: Comparison of Strength Properties of Two Pulping Process for Recycling Shredded Currency Waste into Handmade Paper

S. No.	*Particulars*	*Earlier Process*	*Improved Process*	
		Hydrapulping followed by beating	*Beating*	*Refining*
1.	Tensile Index, Nm/gm	22.85	23.76	24.46
2.	Tear Index, mN.m^2/gm	6.90	7.31	9.54
3.	Burst Index kPa.m^2/gm	1.90	1.93	2.16
4.	Double Fold, No.	30	48	60
5.	Brightness, % ISO	55.0	54.0	54.2

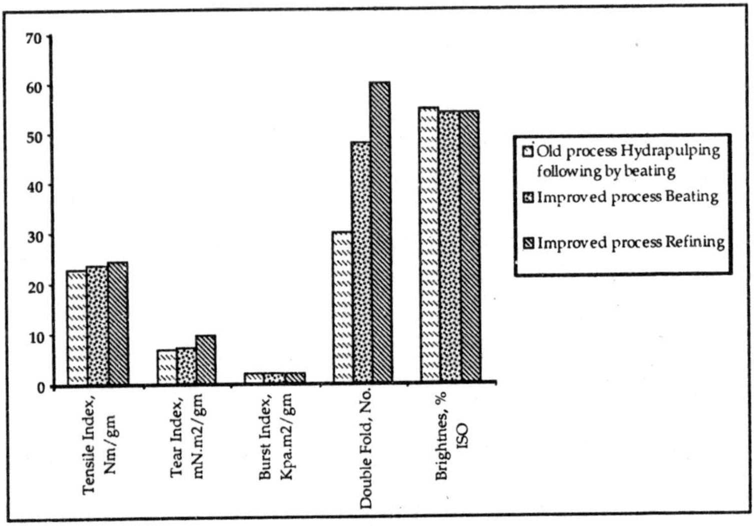

Fig. 16.1: Comparison of the Strength Properties of Shredded Currency Pulp using Two Different Process

Studies on Blending of Shredded Currency Waste Pulp with Mixed Office Waste Pulp

The pulp of shredded currency waste was blended with mixed office waste pulp. The strength properties of the same are placed below in Table 16.5. and Fig. 16.2.

Table 16.5: Strength Properties on Blending of Shredded Currency Waste with Mixed Office Waste Pulp

Particulars	*Improved Process*			
	Beating		*Refining*	
	100% Shred. Curr. waste	*50% Shred. Curr. waste + 50% Office waste*	*100% Shred. Curr. waste*	*50% Shred. Curr. waste + 50% Office waste*
Tensile Index, Nm/gm	23.76	25.10	24.46	26.02
Tear Index, mNm^2/gm	7.31	8.54	9.54	11.54
Burst Index $kpa.m^2/gm$	1.93	2.09	2.16	2.85
Double Fold No.	48	55	60	72
Brightness,% ISO	55.0	58.5	54.2	56.5

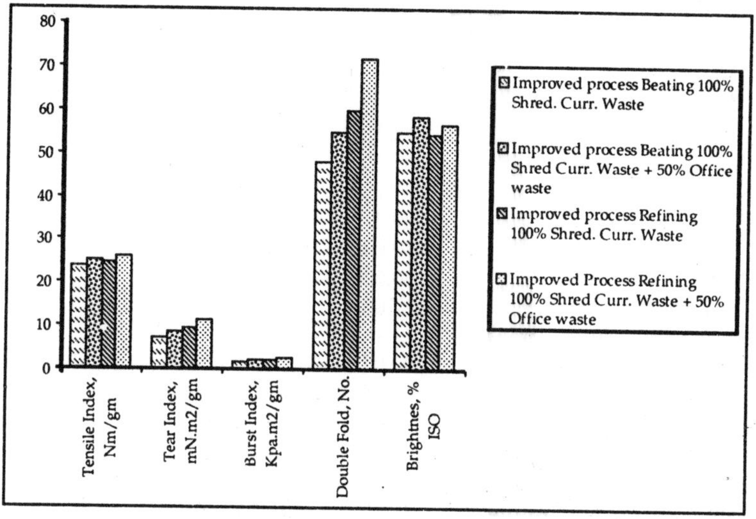

Fig. 16.2: Comparison of Strength Properties of Shredded Currency Pulp using two Different Processes

From the results shown in Table 16.6, it was observed that blending of the pulp of shredded currency waste with mixed office waste pulp could further improve the strength properties in terms of Tensile Index, Tear Index, Burst Index and also Double fold.

Paper Products Made from Recycled Shredded Currency Waste

The handmade paper products that could be made out of handmade paper produced from shredded currency waste are given as below:

- File covers
- Conference folders
- File pads
- Carry bags
- Pamphlet
- Noting sheets
- Office envelopes etc.

Table 16.6: List of Machineries/Equipments Required for Setting up of Handmade Paper Unit Based on Shredded Currency Waste

Earlier Process	*Connected Load, kWh*	*Improved Process*	*Connected Load, kWh*
Pressure Digester	67.50	Pressure Digester	50.62
Non-IBR Boiler	33.75	Non-IBR Boiler	33.75
Potcher washer	39.37	Potcher washer	39.37
Hydra-Pulpur	30.00	Refiner	30.00
Beater	30.00	—	—
Stock chest	27.00	—	—
Hi-density cleaner	—	—	—
Machine chest	30.00	Machine chest	30.00
Johnson vibrating screen	18.00	—	—
Through flow cleaner	39.00	—	—
Cylinder Mould Vat Machine	90.00	Cylinder Mould Vat Machine	90.00
Tentative cost of machinery and equipment Rs. 20,00,000	Total connected load 404.62 kWh	Tentative cost of machinery and equipment Rs. 16,00,000	Total connected load 283.74 kWh

Observations

- Improved strength properties has been achieved in the improved process in comparison to the earlier process. However further increase in strength properties can be achieved by addition of office waste pulp in the pulp of shredded currency waste pulp.
- The improved process gave/paper board at a comparatively cheaper price and improved properties of the handmade paper which can be well utilized for making file covers, carry bags, pamphlets etc.
- There is 75 per cent reduction in energy using refiner in the improved process and if refiner is not available still there is a possibility of saving of nearly 60 per cent energy even with the use of beater.
- Almost 20 per cent less capital investment is required in machinery and equipment in the improved process. The tentative total cost of machinery and equipment

in earlier process is Rs. 20,00,000 while it is only Rs. 16,00,000 in the improved process.

Conclusion

The technology developed for the effective use of shredded currency waste for handmade paper industry has opened new opportunities for the entrepreneurs to switchover to one of the potential raw material in the form of shredded currency waste that is much cheaper and stronger than other prevalent raw materials. It will not only convert waste into wealth but also reduce the pollution load.

17

Role of Kumarappa National Handmade Paper Institute in the Development of Indian Handmade Paper Industry

R.K. JAIN, A.K. SHARMA and SAAKSHY AGARWAL

Introduction

Handmade paper sector is considered to be eco-friendly, utilizing non-woody raw and waste raw materials in its manufacturing process. The durability of the paper is high with exclusive look and texture. The paper is available in a saga of rich varieties, designs, shapes and colours. Most of the handmade paper units in India have been traditionally using cotton hosiery waste as the main source of raw material, which produce paper with excellent strength characteristics. However, increased efficiency of textile mills have resulted in reduced generation and also increased the cost of this raw material. For sustainability of the handmade paper industry in the long run, the use of locally available ligno-cellulosic raw materials may be essential. Further some of these raw materials have been found to impart special characteristics to the paper like strength smoothness etc. which is essential requirement of some of the varieties of handmade paper. The use of these raw materials may also result in increased production at a lower cost. With a small investment, a number of handmade paper making clusters could be developed based on locally available ligno-cellulosic raw materials, namely Jute, Sunn Hemp, Ankara, Bhimal, Banana stem etc. thus solving problem of unemployment, poverty and meeting future demand of paper without effecting the environment. Kumarappa National Handmade Paper Institute since its inception has been engaged in the Research and Development activities for the benefit of Indian Handmade Paper Industry. After exhaustive Research and Development work at the Institute KNHPI has identified number of locally available raw materials and evaluated their potential for handmade paper by developing suitable process technologies for producing varieties of speciality grades of handmade paper. Some of the important ligno cellulosic raw materials studies are Banana fibre, Jute fibre, Sisal fibre, Silk Mulberry, Bhimal fibre, Pineapple etc. Suitability of handmade paper from these fibres has been evaluated on bench as well as pilot scale. Now it is time that these technologies developed by KNHPI are transferred to the handmade paper industry to create confidence among the entrepreneurs and to take full advantage of the technologies developed at KNHPI.

Kumarappa National Handmade Paper Institute (KNHPI)

KNHPI is a world class institute—a centre of excellence in the area of its activities.

The Institute is an autonomous body under KVIC-Ministry of Micro, Small and Medium Enterprises, Government of India engaged in the applied research and development, consultancy and technical services and Human resource and development for the growth of Indian handmade paper industry. The Institute has been working as a torchbearer for the handmade paper industry through its various activities, the most important among them is research and development activities being conducted in the Institute on the various aspects related to handmade paper sector, and for the betterment and upliftment of Indian handmade paper. The research and development activities of the Institute mainly emphasize on exploring various alternative raw materials available abundantly in various regions of the country. The Institute conducts detailed study on utilization of alternative raw materials on laboratory scale and studies its techno-economic feasibility on pilot plant scale. In this line the Institute has further conducted studies on some alternative raw materials and cleaner production technologies for making handmade paper making.

Objectives of the Institute

- To promote the cause of the handmade paper industry.
- Research and other scientific dissemination.
- Transfer of technology connected with the handmade paper industry.
- Maintain laboratories, pilot plant and workshops.
- Human Resource Development in the sector.
- Publication of books, papers and periodicals and scientific data.
- To encourage discoveries, examine and publish information regarding the nature and merits of inventions, improvements, materials and designs.
- To take and acquire patents or licenses relating to such inventions, improvements or processes and to acquire and register designs and standardization marks and to develop, perfect and test their value.

Services Rendered by KNHPI

- Evaluation of alternate fibrous raw materials for their suitability for handmade paper making.
- Testing of papermaking raw materials, pulp paper and boards.
- Consultancy services for the sector on turnkey basis.
- Imparting training for making handmade paper to prospective entrepreneurs and operators.
- Information services on various aspects of the Industry.
- Product development for handmade segment.
- Technology development and trouble shooting services.

ACTIVITIES OF KNHPI

Research & Development Activities

In order to meet the immediate and future requirements of Indian handmade paper industry, the Institute has been focusing its R&D activities in the following areas:

Raw Material and Process Research

Evaluation of Alternative Ligno-Cellulosic Raw Materials

Evaluation of alternative ligno-cellulosic raw materials like Bhimal, Jute, Sunn Hemp, Banana fibre, whole Banana, Banana leaves, Bhang, Ankara, Ramie, Sisal, Daphne paperacea other than conventional raw materials like Hosiery and cotton based raw materials. Some of the work done by this institute has been internationally recognized and acclaimed world premier by eminent expert of international fame.

Development and adoption of environment friendly pulping, bleaching and paper making process.

Cleaner production techniques

- Studies on effluent treatment system.
- Applications of natural dyes in handmade paper industry.
- Biotechnological applications in handmade paper industry.
- Bio-bleaching and bio-retting.

Resource conservation

- Energy conservation studies.
- Water conservation studies.
- Reinforcing recycled fibre (RCF) with hosiery waste.

Product design and development

- Development of acid free paper for archival and other applications.
- Development of electrical insulation paper.
- Development of germination paper.
- Development of handmade paper/board for archival purpose.
- Effective processing of hosiery waste mixed with synthetic fibre (DST project).

Pilot Plant Activities

The research work carried out at laboratory and bench scale is up-scaled to the pilot plant level utilizing the facilities at the Institute.

Production of Blotting Paper/Bond Paper.

Project Consultancy and Technical Services

The Institute provides consultancy and technical services for revival of sick units, de-bottle making, trouble shooting and paper testing services. Following project proposals are in pipe line from different organizations from the various parts of the country in the recent past is placed below:

- Organic waste (garden leaves and banana leaves) for handmade paper/board.
- Shredded currency waste for handmade paper and board.
- Detailed project report prepared for Kreative Handmade Papers, Chennai.
- Effective utilization of synthetic fibre mixed with cotton hosiery.
- Studies on bio-retting of bast fibres for handmade making.
- Utilization of banana leaves/stem fibre for handmade paper.

- Evaluation of possibility of adoption of solar based dryers for drying of handmade paper.

Market research

Studies on development of statistics of Indian Handmade Paper Industry.

Action plan for improved performance of handmade paper industry

Up-gradation of handmade paper clusters: Revival plan for three units along with the detailed project report utilizing shredded currency waste of Reserve Bank of India.

HRD Activities

HRD Programmes and continuing education are important in improving and strengthening the capabilities of Indian handmade paper industry, so that industry could equip itself to compete the changing scenario in the global market. The Institute has been organizing various training programmes such as short-term which involves group training by way of practicals and exposures like orientation training programme for three weeks and specialized operator's training programme of eight weeks for the shop floor people which provides mainly the practical training for the handmade paper and products making. Besides the Institute also conducts one week specialized programme training programme on product design and development covering theoretical as well as practical training.

These programmes have proved to be highly beneficial in skill up-gradation for shop floor people and entrepreneurs and has helped in setting up of various handmade paper units in the country. The training programme is placed as below:

Trg. Courses	*Eligibility*	*Duration*	*Fees (Rs.)*
Orientation Training Programme (OTP)	Graduation	3 Weeks	4000
Specialized Operator Course (SOC)	Matric	8 Weeks	3000
Product Design and Development Programme	Matric	2 Weeks	1000

State-wise Details of Trainees till 2006-07

	OTP	*SOC*	*COC*	*CDP*	*PDD*	*TOTAL*
Andhra Pradesh	29	3	8			40
Arunachal Pradesh	1	2	10			13
Assam	26	0	5		1	32
Bihar	6	0	1			7
Chandigarh	1	1	0			2
Chhattisgarh	1					1
Gujarat	9	3	7			19
Delhi	24	6	1			31
Daman and Diu	1					1
Haryana	18	11	22			51
Himachal Pradesh	1	0	9			10
Jammu & Kashmir	1	0	0			1
Karnataka	7	2	3			12
Kerala	4	0	0			4
Madhya Pradesh	7	2	0			9
Maharashtra	32	5	28			65
Mizoram			4			
Orissa	3	0	1			4
Punjab	6	0	0			6
Rajasthan	170	183	37	9	6	405
Tamil Nadu	7	0	2			9
Tripura	1					1
Uttar Pradesh	37	7	7			51
Uttaranchal	2	0	2		3	7
West Bengal	13	1	5			19
Abroad	7	0	21			28
Total	**414**	**226**	**173**	**9**	**10**	**832**

So far training has been imparted to more than 800 candidates for various parts of the country. Besides the candidates from abroad like Bangladesh, Malawi, US, Ireland, Phillipines and Sri Lanka.

Facilities at KNHPI

The Institute is equipped with state of art sophisticated equipment having divisions as detailed below:

- Chemical and Wet Laboratory
- Physical Laboratory
- Biotech Laboratory
- Pilot Plant
- Product Development Cell
- Human Resource Development
- Information Services
- Consultancy Services

Salient Technological Achievements of KNHPI

- Evaluation of Various Alternative Raw Materials and preparation monograph consisting of evaluation of 16 ligno-cellulosic raw materials.
- Diversified the product range of handmade paper products (marbled papers, algae mottled papers, fancy and decorative papers, carry bags and cards).
- Revival of sick manufacturing units.
- Raising awareness in identifying the role of women in this sub-sector.
- Development and transfer of technology.
- Jute and Jute Waste for handmade paper making.
- Shredded Currency Waste from RBI—DPR prepared and submitted to KVIC for implementation initially in four states.
- Acid free Export-substitute tissue paper from Banana fibre mainly used for conservation purposes.
- Germination paper.
- Utilization of organic waste form of banana leaves from vegetable market—approached Government of Delhi and Rajasthan.
- Utilization of wild Bodha Grass for handmade paper for Department of Forest Andhra Pradesh.

- Development and adoption of Cleaner Production Techniques covering New Pulping Techniques, Natural dyes, Bio-Technological Applications.

Dissemination of Technology

The technologies developed by the institute are disseminated to the handmade paper units through:

- Organization of Workshops at Regional and National levels.
- Quarterly bulletin Hath Kagaz.

Future Prospects of Handmade Paper Industry

We still have to go a long way. The industry has tremendous potential that needs to be exploited. In the context of the changing scenario in the world, because of the day by day growing consciousness on environmental issues such as pollution laws being stringent day by day, banning of usage of plastic bags prohibition of deforestation, fast developing taste for ethnicity and concept of back to basics, the growth of Indian handmade paper industry is expected go up many folds to what it is today. The Indian industry has obvious advantages of cheap labour, cheap and diverse raw materials, creativity and skill. India produces about 50,000 tonnes of handmade paper whereas in China it is 2.0 lakh tonnes.

18

Marketing Potential and Export Opportunities for Indian Handmade Paper Industry

R.K. JAIN and A.K. SHARMA

The Indian handmade paper industry has been identified as one of the village industry and the industry has seen significant growth in last one decade because of improved demand not only on national level but at the international arena. As per estimates, there are nearly more than 450 handmade paper units scattered all over India producing nearly 50,000 tonnes of handmade paper and board. The Indian handmade paper industry had grown remarkably in the recent past wherein the production of handmade paper industry has reached to a turnover of Rs. 250 crores. Indian handmade paper industry contributes to less than 0.5 per cent of the total country's production of paper and paper board till the year 2005-06 and this share has recently increased to nearly 0.7 per cent in the recent year since the production of handmade paper which was nearly 25,000 tonnes in the year 2005-06 now stands at nearly 50,000 tonnes. Although, the country is self sufficient in the manufacturing of handmade paper and board, however, a little quantity of speciality paper are imported.

Indian handmade paper industry is passing through an interesting phase of demand growth both in the domestic and international market. Industrialization has opened up the possibilities of mass production and also generated the mass demand of papers and paper products. The handmade paper industry, which is considered to be ecologically compatible, is a rare blend with enormous potential for creation of much needed additional employment and export. In the present scenario when the developed societies of the world are exploring all possibilities of development through utilization of eco-friendly and bio-degradable products and processes, the Indian handmade paper industry could find good opportunity for higher exports of handmade paper and paper products in global markets.

Table 18.1: Indian Handmade Paper Industry—A Glance

Particulars	*2005-06*	*2006-07*
Estimated Number of Units	450	455
Estimated Production (Tonnes)	25000	50000
Contribution in Total P&B Production %	0.4	0.6
Turnover, Total P&B (Rs. Lakhs)	1800000	2100000
Turnover HMP (Rs. Lakhs)	12500	20000
Total Export P&B (Tonnes)	323000	350000
Exports HMP (Tonnes)	20906	42000
Contribution of Exports of HMP in P&B % (Qty)	6.4	12
Value of Exports Total P&B (Rs. Lakhs)	124639	147500
Value of Exports of HMP (Rs. Lakhs)	7723	15717
Contribution of Exports of HMP in P&B (Value)	6.2	10.7
Imports HMP (Tonnes)	3755	2800
Value of Imports of HMP (Rs. Lakh)	847.7	518.6

Demand and Supply

The paper has become an indispensable commodity in our day to day life, in every field whether it is writing, reading and displaying science and technology or in any other industrial use. Due to increased literacy rate and industrialization, the per capita consumption of paper in India has increased from 4 kgs. in 1990 to 7 kgs. in the recent time. As per estimates, it is presumed that the requirement of paper is likely to increase manifold due to the various programme initiated by government to improve literacy and certainly the handmade paper could be a major contributor to this increased demand of the country.

Before 1991 the industry was heavily dependent on captive market, *i.e.* supply to State Government and Central Government against reservations. The shift started taking place in this scenario after 1991. Since 1991 the handmade paper industry in the country increased more than 100 per cent and in the export sector an impressive 1000 per cent increase has been noticed.

The situation has entirely changed and the industry has found many other end-users including penetration in the international market in a big way. This situation has resulted in enhancement in capacity utilization, product diversification, culture of competitiveness, better management and market approach.

Handmade paper production meets only 0.5 per cent of India's total requirement of paper. It has been observed that there is much scope of bridging the gap by exploring more potential of handmade paper in domestic market by decreasing its cost and adopting intermediate technology. The handmade paper and its allied products offers a vast marketing scope in both domestic and export market.

For marketing of its various products, the handmade paper industry can develop the linkages and sell their items to the following clientelle:

Domestic Market Scenario

The relative strength of the handmade paper industry like opportunity of employment generation, ecological considerations, investment criteria, durability, strength and permanency of the product needs to be supplemented with status symbol of the user of the handmade paper, the planners and policy-makers. The customers education awareness about its relative strength and regularity of supply with quality control assumes great significance.

Captive Market

Domestic market presents divergent scenario with persistent and sustained demand for quality products on one hand and scarcity of such products on the other hand. Domestic market of handmade paper has been developed mainly by efforts of KVIC, KVIB and some private dealers, stationary dealers and the production units themselves. As per the estimates, the requirement of paper and board by Central and State Government/PSU's works out to be around 7 lakhs tonnes. Even the specific items that can be supplied by handmade paper sector accounts for 10 per cent of the same, the handmade paper industry has to step up its production manifold.

This would not only help all existing units to work round the clock but would also have the way for the growth of units in the sector.The private market/open market has tremendous demand which is growing for the converted items like letter head pads, visiting cards, greeting cards, invitation cards required by large corporate houses, big hotels, PSU's banks etc. Concerted efforts are required to streamline the production and supply of handmade paper of uniform quality and standards to convert it into value added products and provide enough margin to the production units.

Non-Captive Market

Non-captive market needs to be developed to give handmade paper industry a boost. This is the most competitive and quality conscious market. Prompt services and perfect quality control are the pre-requisite to any approach adopted for developing this market. Non-captive market includes both institutional and non-institutional segments.

International Market

The Indian handmade paper industry has made big dent in the international market. The Indian handmade paper and the value added product of the handmade paper have made a quantum jump. The value added products has a major share. According to an estimate it is more than 70 per cent of the total exports. The Indian converters have become more innovative and learnt the art of product development according to changing taste of the customers and fashion abroad with design inputs for both functional and decorative purposes. The products of handmade paper are exported as handicraft products. A number of handmade paper units have set up their own in-house facility for conversion and value addition. They are export oriented units.

As per one estimate, nearly 75 per cent Handmade Paper Produced in India is exported to various countries. Export of handmade paper has increased about 10 times in the last five years which has increased from 2000 tonnes (1999-2000) to 20900 tonnes (2005-06). The volume of imports has been low; however, there has been an upsurge in the last fiscal, the major import coming from USA and UAE, which is a change in trend from Nepal and Netherlands/Malaysia. The major countries of exports of handmade paper are Nigeria, Sri Lanka, Egypt Malaysia, Kenya, Bangladesh and European Union. However, there is quantum jump in export as shown in data given below which clearly indicated that export of handmade paper and paper board during the year 2006-07 has been doubled as against the quantity exported in 2005-06 as given in Table 18.2.

Table 18.2: Handmade Paper—Existing Export Markets

Country	*2004-05*		*2005-06*		*2006-07*	
	Qty. (Ton)	*Value (Lac)*	*Qty. (Ton)*	*Value (Lac)*	*Qty. (Ton)*	*Value (Lac)*
Nigeria	3130	862	6306	2034	14109	4752
Sri Lanka	3851	1127	3152	865	5196	1945
Ecuador	0		0		2500	820
USA	182	137	182	223	610	776
Guatemala	0		0		2272	745
Kenya	319	96	554	181	1914	606
Yemen	473	158	85	71	1890	585
UK	121	95	122	136	1177	696
UAE	415	134	406	141	1123	407
Malaysia	1910	567	2127	645	951	304
Egypt	1881	507	2211	568	783	257
Djibouti	174	55	505	207	760	284
Dominican	0		0		574	185
Thailand	602	167	12	12	569	179
Sudan	297	87	529	163	498	176
Turkey	597	153	16	5	418	132
Ethiopia	384	107	797	268	395	108
Panama	0		1	0	247	79
Ghana	550	178	252	81	218	71
Germany	41	63	92	127	209	385
Total	**14928**	**4493**	**17349**	**5727**	**36413**	**13490**
World	**19370**	**6107**	**19445**	**7310**	**38866**	**14896**

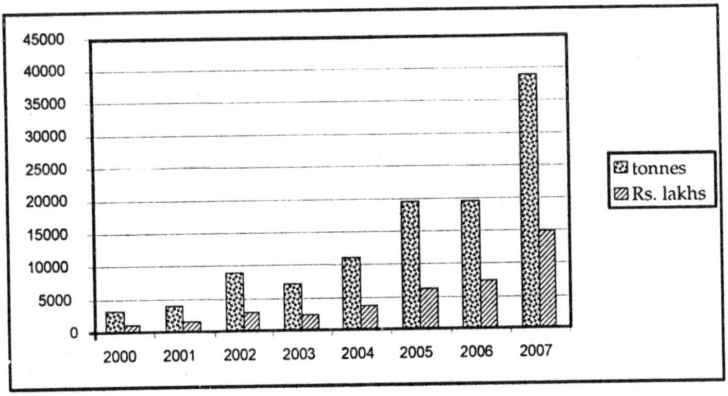

Handmade Paper

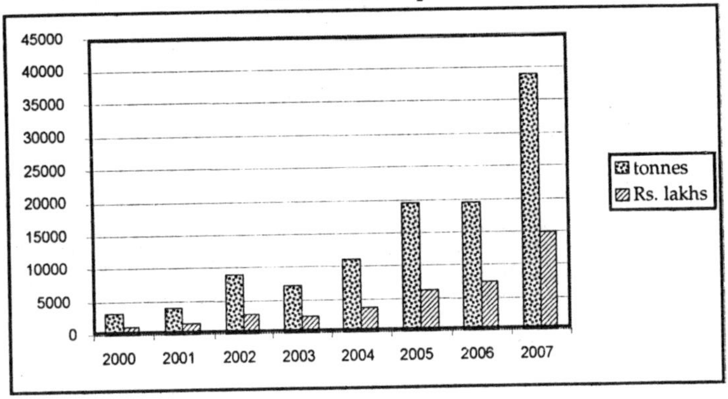

Handmade Paper Board

Fig. 18.1: Export of Handmade Paper and Paper Board—Trends

Issues, Strengths and Opportunities to Boost Marketing of Indian Handmade Paper Industry

In the rapidly changing economic environment, certain issues are confronting with the handmade paper industry needs to be addressed to promote and develop the sector. With the opening of the global economy, the competitiveness of the paper industry including the handmade paper has came to a sharp focus. This means handmade paper industry has to focus its attention to produce better products, more value addition and easily availability through wide marketing network and better servicing. Modernization does not mean only technological betterment but also learning modern methods of cost effectiveness, marketing and value addition of products.

Raw material availability

The global crisis regarding the ill effects of deforestation and environmental pollution demands, a system of living conducive to healthy maintenance of eco-system and limiting industrialization to an optimal and essential level. To produce one tonne of mill made paper, it requires to cut nearly 300 trees of eucalyptus or 500 plants of bamboo besides consumption of enormous quantities of hazardous chemicals, thermal and electrical energy, water discharged in the form of effluents thereby causing severe problem of water and air pollution.

Scarce availability and rising demand and cost of traditionally used raw material hosiery waste has forced the industry to search for alternative and cost effective ligno-cellulosic raw materials. Based on the extensive research work carried out at KNHPI, large number of exciting possibilities are now available in the shape of Sunn Hemp, Sisal, Banana, Aakra, Jute and Bhimal etc. Possibililty of utilization of these raw materials has offered potential for availability of low cost good quality cellulosic raw materials thereby imparting the cost effectiveness of the product.

Product Development and Diversification

Majority of handmade paper unit produces paper in sheet form and utilize it for stationary and related applications. There is an increasing trend of value added articles such as drying blocks for art work, letter heads with matching eve, greeting card in attractive shades and design, paper carry bags, deckle edge drawing paper and bond paper, fancy and decorative stationary paper and decorative paper bags in the export markets like US, Germany, Canada and other countries.

The vast potential exists for product development and diversification, therefore, the activities of product design and development needs to be addressed:

(a) In promoting production of these converted items having high value addition.
(b) In bringing design and managerial skills not only to cater the diverse requirement of market but to ensure that the value added items are developed and produced keeping in mind the inherent strength of material.
(c) To offer an eco-friendly alternatives like cost effective carry bags.

ISO Certification and Eco-labelling

Handmade paper units should acquire ISO certification since ISO standards are globally acceptable. Environmental standards and method of assessing compliance to their requirement normally issued by an independent certification organization. Eco-labelling attempts to encourage the manufacturing of products with a reduced impact on the environment and to address public concern about raw material scarcity, shrinking landfill space and impact on pollutants on air and water. Indian handmade paper industry should promote the special eco-friendly characteristics of Indian handmade paper and its products conforming to similar standards in Europe, US and Canada which should boost its marketing potential in global market.

To encash the credibility of eco-friendly characteristics of handmade paper, there is a need to:

- have separate commodity code under ITC-HS classification so that all the converted items from handmade paper could be exported under specified code and have its identity being eco-lable and environment friendly.
- to have a recognized laboratory like KNHPI equipped with facilities to test and certify that the paper is handmade and free from toxic chemicals like azo dyes and unfriendly materials and processes.

Various eco-labels used worldwide

German blue eco-label: The world first eco-labelling programme created in 1977 to promote environment friendly products and cover 4000 products.

European Eco-label: Launched in 1992, the label is awarded to product that have a reduced impact environment.

Environment choice programme of Canada: Created in 1988.

Sustainable Forest Management (SFM): Recently introduced in Canada.

Indian handmade paper industry should also insist on creating similar eco-labels.

KNHPI's Role in Development of Handmade Paper Industry

Kumarappa National Handmade Paper Institute has been working as a torchbearer for the handmade paper industry through its various activities, the most important among these are the research and development activities carried out for growth and development of the Indian handmade paper industry. Through its various programmes the Institute has been engaged in various activities placed as below:

- Enhancing the performance of Indian handmade paper industry to improve its competitiveness in domestic as well as global market by development of new alternative raw materials, process know how for pulping and paper making employing environmental friendly technologies.
- Identification of product preferences in domestic and international market and providing assistance for its production.
- Providing technical consultancy for trouble shooting and revival of sick and dormant handmade paper units thereby improving competitiveness and sustainability.
- Human resource development through training.
- Dissemination of information about the technological developments through organization of exhibitions, workshops and seminars.
- The above activities have helped the industry to improve its productivity, quality, cost effectiveness and marketability of the products in the domestic and global market.

Conclusion

Growth prospects are excellent and future is bright for Indian handmade paper industry. Search for alternative raw materials, product design and diversification and the concept of environment friendliness and eco-labelling could be the key driver for demand and growth in the domestic and export market. The wide gap between domestic consumption of handmade paper and machine made could be abridged by cost-effective production using alternative raw materials and new process technologies thereby, providing opportunities for employment generation.

Acknowledgement

The authors express their gratitude to Ms. Saakshy Agarwal, Scientist KNHPI for the support in preparation of the manuscripts of the article and data compilation.

19

Indian Handmade Paper Industry
Prospects and Perspectives

R.K. JAIN and A.K. SHARMA

Handmade Paper Industry—A Road Map

The history of paper dates back to the history of human culture and civilization. The Egyptians, Greeks and Romans wrote on "Papyrus", a paper—like material. Today's kind of paper was first developed and used in China. Since its birth the paper was the most important carrier of information in the past. Growth of population and need to transfer the knowledge, education and information to the society at large were the forcing factors for stupendous increase in the production of paper. In former times paper was a valuable product and paper making an art—that was often kept secret because of the outstanding advantages of the product.

Milestone of the history of paper making is shown in Fig. 19.1. The history of handmade paper in India dates back to the 3rd century BC. Making handmade paper is a traditional art that has been practiced by a particular class of people for generations together. This art has been passed on from one generation of craftsmen to another. These craftsmen are known as "Kagzi's". Their name is derived from the Urdu word 'kavas', which means paper. The size of this community has dwindled over the years. There is a small settlement of "Kagzi's" in Sanganer near Jaipur, where a section of this community settled thousands of years ago. They claim that they are originally from Turkey and from there moved to China and then finally settled in India.

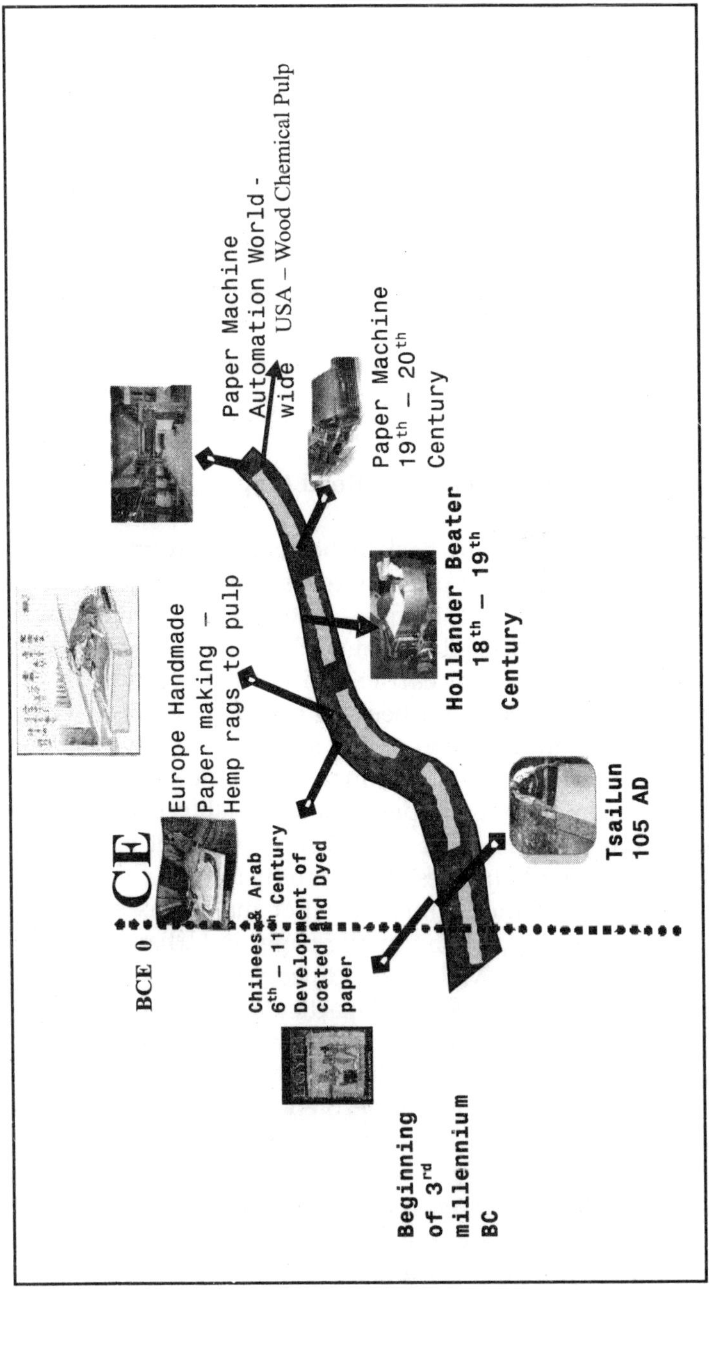

Fig. 19.1: Milestones of Handmade Paper Industry

In Sanganer the 'Kagzi' community is the primary owner of the handmade paper industry in the town. Their history goes back to the 14th century when the ruler was Feroze Shah Tughlaq. Even in those days the royalty used handmade paper made by them for official documents, miniature paintings, calligraphy, and to make copies of the Holy Quran and to maintain account books. In the 16th century the then ruler of Amber, Raja Man Singh brought the Kagzis to Sanganer and settled them on the bank of the river Saraswati, where clean water was easily available. Thus the town emerged as one of the biggest paper producing centres in north India.

Under the British handmade paper received a serious setback as the British encouraged the import of mill-made paper from the Western countries. By the 1930s there were only a handful of people from this community practicing their traditional trade. At this point, Mahatma Gandhi provided them with the much-needed support by buying handmade paper in bulk for his Ashram and other associates. After independence, the Khadi and Village Industries Commission (KVIC) included handmade paper in the list of crafts to be promoted. Over the years the handmade paper industry has grown slowly but steadily and is today a major player in the world market, exporting a major portion of its production.

Status of Handmade Paper Industry in India

The Indian handmade paper industry has been identified as one of the village industry and the industry has seen significant growth in last one decade because of improved demand not only on national level but at the international arena. As per estimates, there are nearly more than 450 handmade paper units scattered all over India producing nearly 50,000 tonnes of handmade paper and board. The Indian handmade paper industry had grown remarkably in the recent past wherein the production of handmade paper industry has reached to a turnover of Rs. 250 crores.

Due to increased literacy, industrialization and modernization, the per capita consumption of the paper and paper board has increased remarkably from 4.5 kg. in the year

2000 to nearly 6.5 kg. in the recent past. This industry provides employment to about 10,000 people and most of them are situated in the rural areas. Although, the per capita consumption of paper and paper board in India is low compared to the developed countries like US (350 kg.), China (58 kgs.), Japan (225 kgs.) and world average 55 kgs. However the total quantity of paper produced in India is quite significant with a total production of nearly 70 lakh tonnes per annum.

Table 19.1: Indian Handmade Paper Industry—A Glance

Particulars	*2005-06*	*2006-07*
Estimated Number of Units	450	455
Estimated Production (Tonnes)	25000	50000
Contribution in Total P&B Production %	0.4	0.6
Turnover, Total P&B (Rs. Lakhs)	1800000	2100000
Turnover HMP (Rs. Lakhs)	12500	20000
Total Export P&B (Tonnes)	323000	350000
Exports HMP (Tonnes)	20906	42000
Contribution of Exports of HMP in P&B % (Qty)	6.4	12
Value of Exports Total P&B (Rs. Lakhs)	124639	147500
Value of Exports of HMP (Rs. Lakhs)	7723	15717
Contribution of Exports of HMP in P&B % (Value)	6.2	10.7
Imports HMP (Tonnes)	3755	2800
Value of Imports of HMP (Rs. Lakhs)	847.7	518.6

Indian handmade paper industry contributes to less than 0.5 per cent of the total country's production of paper and paper board till the year 2005-06 and this share has recently increased to nearly 0.7 per cent in the recent year since the production of handmade paper which was nearly 25,000 tonnes in the year 2005-06 now stands at nearly 50,000 tonnes. Although, the country is self sufficient in the manufacturing of handmade paper and board, however, a little quantity of speciality paper are imported.

Raw Material Scenario—Research and Development Work at Kumarappa National Handmade Paper Institute (KNHPI)

Handmade paper in India is made by recycling waste materials like cotton rags from hosiery cuttings and small amounts of waste paper. However, increased efficiency of textile mills have resulted in reduced generation and also increased the cost of this raw material.

For sustainability of the Indian handmade paper industry, the use of locally available ligno-cellulosic raw materials may be essential. Further, some of these raw materials have been found to impart special characteristics to the paper like strength smoothness etc. which is essential requirement of some of the varieties of handmade paper. The use of these raw materials may also result in increased production at a lower cost.

With a small investment, a number of handmade paper making clusters could be developed based on locally available ligno-cellulosic raw materials, namely Jute, Sunn Hemp, Ankara, Bhimal, Banana stem etc. thus solving problem of unemployment, poverty and meeting future demand of paper without effecting the environment. Agro fibres like jute, straw, banana are added to the primary fibre to create mottled handmade paper. Handmade paper has greater tensile, bursting, tearing and double fold strength when compared with conventional mill-made paper. It does not turn become brittle as it ages. Besides, handmade paper is attractive and exclusive. The paper is available in a saga of rich varieties, designs, shapes and colours.

KNHPI—Since its inception has been engaged in the Research and Development activities for the growth of Indian handmade paper Industry. After exhaustive Research and Development work at the Institute KNHPI , a number of locally available ligno-cellulosic raw materials have been identified and evaluated for their utilization in handmade paper making. The Institute has developed the ecological compatible pulping, bleaching and paper making processes employing the use of natural dyes and biotechnological applications which could result in the production of speciality grades of handmade papers which could be labelled as eco-friendly paper finding lot of demand for exports in developed countries like USA, European Union and other countries. Some of the important ligno-cellulosic raw materials studies are Banana fibre, Jute fibre, Sisal fibre, Silk Mulberry, Bhimal fibre, Pine apple etc. Suitability of handmade paper from these fibres has been evaluated on bench as well as pilot scale. Now it is time that these technologies developed by KNHPI are transferred to the handmade paper industry to create confidence among the entrepreneurs and to take full advantage of the technologies developed at KNHPI.

Location of Handmade Paper Clusters in India

There are number of cluster of handmade paper units existed in different parts of the country in states like Uttar Pradesh, Rajasthan, Haryana, Andhra Pradesh, Karnataka and North East which provide certain advantage of the common facilities to these units, the details of the cluster is shown in Fig. 19.2.

Demand and Supply

The paper has become an indispensable commodity in our day to day life, in every field whether it is writing, reading and displaying science and technology or in any other industrial use. Due to increased literacy rate and industrialization, the per capita consumption of paper in India has increased from 4 kgs. in 1990 to 7 kgs. in the recent time. As per estimates, it is presumed that the requirement of paper is likely to be increased manifold due to the various programmes initiated by government to improve literacy and certainly the handmade paper could be a major contributor to this increased demand of the country.

Before 1991 the industry was heavily dependent on captive market, *i.e.* supply to State Government and Central Government against reservations. The shift started taking place in this scenario after 1991. Since 1991 the handmade paper industry in the country increased more than 100 per cent and in the export sector an impressive 1000 per cent increase has been noticed.

The situation has entirely changed and the industry has found many other end-users including penetration in the international market in a big way. This situation has resulted in enhancement in capacity utilization, product diversification, culture of competitiveness, better management and market approach.

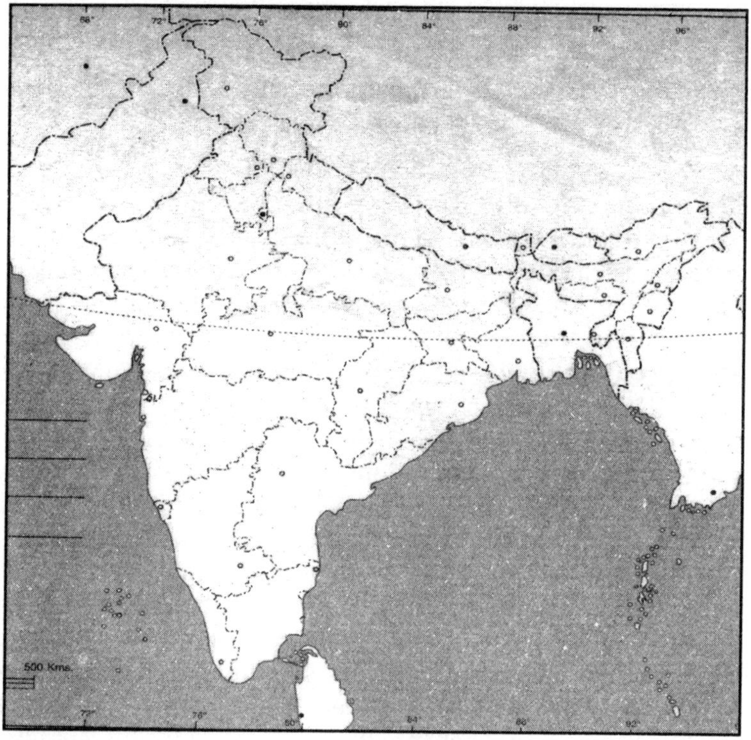

Cities
Kalpi—50
Sanganer—75
Kurukshetra—25
Pune—20
Mehboob Nagar
and
Kareem Nagar—12

State
Karnataka—10
Tripura—5
Gujarat—5

Fig. 19.2: Handmade Paper Clusters in India

Handmade paper production meets only 0.5 per cent of India's total requirement of paper. It has been observed that there is much scope of bridging the gap by exploring more potential of handmade paper in domestic market by decreasing its cost and adopting intermediate technology. The handmade paper and its allied products offers a vast marketing scope in both domestic and export market.

For marketing of its various products, the handmade paper industry can develop the linkages and sell their items to the following clienteles:

Domestic Market

The present domestic market presents divergent scenario with persistent and sustained demand for quality products on one hand and scarcity of such quality items on the other Central Government and State Government are main purchasers of file covers, flaps, file boards etc. Government of India reserved 50 per cent to purchase file cover and office stationary from KVIC/KVIB units which is to be implemented in an organized way. If only 10 per cent of this supply is reserved for handmade paper industries, it will be about 7 times the present quantum of production. Besides, there is the non-captive market which can be classified into institutional and non-institutional. Institutional market demands bigger quantities while non-institutional smaller. There are the eco-conscious buyers who purchase environment friendly produces to enhance its image. There are the quality conscious buyers who purchase handmade paper for its exclusiveness in texture, long lasting quality and beauty. There are the price conscious buyers who purchase handmade paper because it is cheaper than mill made products for some varieties.

Export Market

The demand for handmade paper and its allied products is gradually increasing not only in the domestic market but also in the export market. For the last two decades the handmade paper industry has been exporting certain exclusive varieties like deckle edge stationary drawing paper, marble paper, mottle paper made from jute, wool, algae, straw, grass etc. and recorded significant growth in the export sector. Foreign buyers like US, Germany, UK, Canada, Italy, Sweden, Australia, Singapore and Hong Kong are purchasing handmade paper from India because handmade paper production in India by all means is as low as compared to the production areas abroad.

Now foreign buyers are purchasing handmade paper due to increasing environment awareness.

As per one estimate, nearly 75 per cent Handmade Paper produced in India is exported to various countries. Export of handmade Paper has increased about 10 times in the last five years which has increased from 2000 tonnes (1999-2000) to 20900 tonnes (2005-06). The volume of imports has been low; however, there has been an upsurge in the last fiscal, the major import coming from USA and UAE, which is a change in trend from Nepal and Netherlands/Malaysia. The major countries of exports of handmade paper are Nigeria, Sri Lanka, Egypt Malaysia, Kenya, Bangladesh and European Union. However, there is quantum jump in export as shown in data given below which clearly indicated that export of handmade paper and paper board during the year 2006-07 has been doubled as against the quantity exported in 2005-06 as given in Table 19.1.

Table 19.1: Export of Handmade Paper and Paper Board

Year	*Quantity of export of hand-made paper (Tonnes)*	*Value of exports of hand-made made (Rs. Lac)*	*Quantity of export of total paper and paper board*	*Value of exports of total paper and paper board (Rs. Lac)*	*% share in value hand-made paper in total export*	*% share in quantity of hand-made paper in total export*
2000-01	4194	1568	1,98,000	73215	2.14	2.11
2001-02	5197	2096	224000	76218	2.75	2.32
2002-03	10,170	3332	272000	101357	3.28	3.73
2003-04	14,369	4684	233000	81327	5.75	6.16
2004-05	21,800	6890	281000	103594	6.65	7.75
2005-06	20,906	7723	323000	124639	6.19	6.47
2006-07	42000	15717	350000	147500	10.06	12.00

Prospects for Indian Handmade Paper Industry

The future of the handmade paper industry is bright and its growth-prospects are excellent due to the product character which enthralls eco-friendly nature of the product. The concept of environmental friendliness deserves this product to become taste worthy to the customer. No deforestation takes place. Water and air pollution is also negligible. The export of handmade paper has a great potential. The demand of handmade paper is increasing day by day in the domestic market also. As the demand increases need for meeting the supply also increases.

Since handmade paper production in India meets only 0.5 per cent of the total requirement of paper, there exist a lot of potential of growth of handmade paper industry by replacing the demand of machine made paper with handmade paper. The gap can be abridged by lowering the cost of production of handmade paper by producing different grades of paper, adopting new technologies, utilizing alternative raw materials, improving the quality of the products and providing gainful employment.

Acknowledgement

The authors express their gratitude to Ms. Saakshy Agarwal, Scientist KNHPI in preparation of the manuscripts of the article and data compilation.

REFERENCES

Handmade paper history.htm

India handmade paper-Arts-Terra India_Knolwdege India.htm

Presentation delivered by Dr. R.K. Jain on "Overview of Kumarappa National Handmade Paper Institute and its Role in the progress of Indian Handmade Paper" during visit of Hon'ble cabinet Minister Shri Mahaveer Prasad Ji on 7th July 2007.

20

Bioretting in the Context of Handmade Paper Industry

R.K. JAIN, A.K. SHARMA and SUNITA CHAUHAN

Introduction

The rapidly changing economic and environmental needs of the society are putting ever increasing pressure on the forests-based industry *"To do more with less"*. This means increasing the conversion of an efficient use of the available fibre resources producing more fibre on a shrinking land base using environmentally friendly processes and technologies and also more and more use of the non-woody ligno-cellulosic fibres for industrial products.

Continuously increasing demand and rising cost of traditionally used cellulosic raw materials by handmade paper industry like hosiery waste/cotton rags has forced the industry to look for alternate and locally available non-woody ligno-cellulosic raw materials with the application of environmental friendly processes.

As a part of promotion of the green and clean technologies, Kumarappa National Handmade Paper Institute (KNHPI) focused its research and development activities in the area of identification of alternate ligno-cellulosic raw materials with integration of biotechnological approach employing identified micro-organisms and/or enzymes suitable for specific applications.

The initiatives taken at KNHPI for utilization of widely available raw materials like *Calotropis procera (Ankara), Bhimal* etc. in the area of fibre extraction using bioretting process developed at the institute and utilization of the extracted fibre for making handmade paper and products should prove to be a potential employment generating and income generating opportunity among the rural masses. Proper utilization of the waste biomass, majority of which is presently utilized as a domestic fuel, could also improve the environmental status besides addressing the problem of Global warming.

Need of Alternative Sources of Raw Materials and Ecologically Compatible Procedures for their Use: In the present context of environmental friendliness, consumers are inclining towards handmade paper and with the increasing demand, more and more of handmade paper units are coming up in the country. To satisfy the raw material requirement of all these units, cotton rags or hosiery waste (traditionally used raw material) are getting inadequate and costlier too. Therefore, Indian handmade paper industry has been confronting with various challenges of which availability of good quality cellulosic raw materials in a sustainable way is one of the major challenges. Search for alternative ligno-cellulosic raw materials, which are locally available, has therefore become an area of research and interest. Use of these alternative ligno-cellulosic raw materials, which basically involve bast and leaf fibres may include chemicals during pulping and bleaching processes for effective delignification, required for producing quality handmade paper. On contrary to this, the traditionally used raw materials like cotton hosiery waste and cotton rags do not require any chemicals during pulping thereby retaining eco-friendly status. In order to retain the eco-friendly credentials of the handmade paper industry, there is an urgent need to develop ecologically compatible processes for pulping and bleaching these alternative ligno-cellulosic raw materials. In pursuit of developing such techniques by KNHPI, biotechnology covering enzymatic prebleaching of pulp using xylanase and laccases, enzymatic retting, bio-refining and biopulping could found to be one of the potential options for its applications in handmade paper sector.

The present paper narrates about the process of bioretting in the specific context of handmade paper industry. Bioretting is highly significant in the present scenario because with the inclination of consumers towards handmade papers made out of natural fibres, there is a need of the consistent supply of the natural fibres in an economical way. The locally available and easily pulpable sources of ligno-cellulosic raw materials like banana, jute, silk mulberry (*Moru alba*), paper mulberry (*Broussentia papyrifera*) etc. are some of the good options to make handmade papers out of natural fibres. Since the quality of handmade paper produced from the fibre extracted from the ligno-cellulosic raw materials is found to be superior in terms of physicochemical and strength properties, which could find applications in value added products, the extraction of fibre from these plant materials is an important process in the present context.

Review of Literature

Plant Fibres and their Extraction: Plant fibres are long, narrow, thick-walled and lignified sclerenchymatous cells, which are dead and therefore serve the purely mechanical function of giving strength and rigidity to the plant body. Plant fibres are classified into three main types according to their origin and structure: **surface fibre**, which is produced on the surface of stems, leaves etc. *e.g.* cotton (*Gossypium* sp.); **hard** or **structural fibres**, which are supportive and conductive fibro vascular bundles, chiefly found in monocots *e.g.* Manilla hemp (Musa textiles) and **soft** or **bast fibres**, formed in groups outside xylem in the cortex, phloem or pericycle *e.g.* Ramie, Jute, paper mulberry, sunn hemp etc. The plant fibres like banana, jute, paper mulberry etc. are very useful for making different varieties of handmade papers.

Conventional Process of Fibre Extraction: The process of extracting fibre from non-fibre tissue is called retting. Retting is a microbial process that breaks the chemical bonds holding the stem together and allows separation of the bast fibres from the woody core (Danny, E.A. and *et al.* 2000). The process of retting is being utilized for centuries in traditional ways for extracting the fibre. There are mainly four kinds of retting processes (Chauhan, S. 2004) which are:

1. Dew or field retting
2. Pool-retting
3. Stream retting
4. Water retting

1. Dew or Field Retting

This is the oldest technique as retting of green and dried flax was used by the Egyptians thousands of years ago. Under this technique, plant stems are cut or pulled up and left in the field to rot by exposure to dew, rain, wind and sunlight. The process is to be monitored closely to ensure that the bast fibres separate from the inner core without much deterioration in quality. Moisture is needed for the microbial breakdown to occur but then the weather must be dry for bailing. It is an inexpensive, mechanized procedure and does not use water. But it causes large variations in fibre quality; coarser and lower quality of fibre than with water-retting, it has limitation to geographical regions with appropriate temperature and moisture, High labour costs and occupation of agricultural land for several weeks.

2. Pool-Retting (Blue-Ret/Green-Ret)

This method was also used by ancient Egyptians and described by Pliny (79 A.D.). It is one of the most rapid natural retting procedures. According to this method, flax, tied up as beets was used to be lowered into the pool, weighed down with sods to keep it under water and the micro-organisms retted the flax within 1-3 weeks. This method in use until 1920, produced fibres with a grayish-blue appearance. So, it is also known as blue-ret or green ret.

3. Stream Retting (Analogous to Pool-Retting)

In this type of retting, flax was used to be submerged in slow running water, which does not contain as many bacteria as stagnant water. The method was used in Netherlands and Germany. Due to the negative side effects, it was abandoned in 1937-1943. Despite the enormous economic benefits, it has disadvantages of river pollution, a sour, unpleasant smell and navigational problems.

4. Water Retting

In principle, the method is analogous to stream-retting but the stems are retted for 4-7 days depending on the quality of the plant used in heated tanks or pits maintained at 40 °C. Warm water retting which can be used all year round, results normally in finer fibres of better quality than those produced by dew-retting. Although it produces more uniform and high-quality fibre yet the stench from fermentation by anaerobic bacteria and the resulting stench-tainted fibres and high labour costs prevent it from being used widely today. It has been largely abandoned in countries where strict environmental regulations exist because of the environmentally unacceptable fermentation waste.

Thus the traditional retting process is quite tedious which involves treatment of the woody raw material under water in submerged conditions over a long period of 15-30 days and which also results in inferior quality fibre and creates problem of water pollution besides concern for global warming. So, an alternative method of fibre extraction is the need of the hour.

The bast fibres like ramie thus obtained are good natural textile material or papermaking raw materials but decorticated ramie or other such fibres contain 20-30 per cent ramie gum, which consists mainly of pectic and hemicelluloses and degumming is necessary to meet textile or other industrial requirements. Therefore, prior to industrial utilization of the processed bast fibres, removal of heavily coated, non-cellulosic gummy material from the cellulosic part of fibres *i.e.* "degumming" is necessary. In the classical degumming process, the heavy coating of gums, waxes and pectin that remains on the processed bast fibres. On an industrial scale, the degumming of bast fibres is carried out by treating the crude fibres with dilute *lye* solutions (12-20% NaOH and 2% NaOH in case of ramie and sunn hemp respectively) containing wetting and reducing agents. Following a 24 hrs. soaking period, the fibres are boiled for 1-4 h, rinsed, neutralized, washed and centrifuged several times. The fibres are then dried over charcoal fire and treated with softeners such as glycerine, wax, soap etc. to prevent the fibres from becoming brittle. The cleaned fibres are further graded and processed.

The chemical treatment of fibres is believed to produce polluting, toxic and non-biodegradable effluents and causes serious environmental threats and biological disturbances, not to mention the high consumption of energy. With rising energy costs due to scarcity of energy resources, and deterioration of the environment beyond a tolerable level, there is an urgent need to develop alternate, environmentally friendly processes for degumming and processing of bast fibres.

Bioretting or Enzymatic Retting or Enzymatic Method of Fibre Extraction: To overcome the handicaps of dew and water retting, a new method of enzymatic retting or bioretting has been developed. It produces a better quality of fibre in higher yield and consistent quality. Moreover, it is faster than traditional retting, readily controlled and produces fewer odours.

Bioretting process, which involves the use of pectinase-based enzymes; holds greater promise for extraction of fibre. In the process of bioretting or enzymatic retting, the microbial enzymes produced by the retting agents during dew retting or in warm water retting are replaced by the industrially obtained enzymes mainly pectinases. Pectic substances are ubiquitous in the plant kingdom and form the major components of middle lamella, a thin layer of adhesive extracellular material found between the primary cell walls of adjacent young plant cells. The enzymes hydrolyzing these pectic substances are broadly known as pectinases and include polygalacturonases, pectin esterases, pectin lyases and pectate lyases depending on their mode of action. Pectolysis is one of the most important processes for plants as it plays a role in cell elongation and growth as well as in fruit ripening. Pectolytic enzymes are widespread in nature and are produced by bacteria, fungi, yeasts, insects, nematodes and protozoa. Microbial pectolysis is important in plant pathogenesis, symbiosis and plant deposits. Thus by breaking down pectin polymer for nutritional purposes, microbial pectolytic enzymes play a hugely important role in nature. Pectinases are produced from a wide variety of microbial sources such as bacteria, yeast, fungi and actinomycetes.

Role of Pectinases in Bioretting Process

The biotechnological potential of pectinolytic enzymes from micro-organisms has drawn a great deal of attention from various researchers worldwide as likely biological catalysts in a variety of industrial processes. Alkaline pectinases are among the most important industrial enzymes and are of great significance in the current biotechnological arena with wide ranging applications in textile processing, degumming of plant bast fibres, treatment of pectic wastewaters, papermaking and coffee and tea fermentations.

The most upcoming application of pectolytic enzymes is their use in the degumming and extraction of plant fibres such as ramie, sunn hemp, jute, flax and hemp. Polysaccharide-degrading microorganisms and enzymes such as pectinases or a combination of pectinases and xylanases could be used to remove the gummy material from plant fibres. The processing of fibre is fast and degumming is much more specific.

Pectins which are chemically complex binding substances in plants, hold fibres in bundles and the bundles between non-fibre tissues in the outer region of the stems. While most enzymes for retting purpose are mixtures of polysacchari-disases, pectinases are essential for effective retting and constitute a large proportion of successful retting formulation. Pectinases are believed to play a leading role in the processing of fibres, since 40 per cent of dry weight of plant cambium cells is comprised of pectin. Pectinases effectively assist in degumming, maceration and retting of jute, flax, hemp and ramie bast fibres by degrading the pectin located in the middle lamella and primary cell wall.

Commercial enzymes such as cellulases, hemicellulases, pectinases and other polysaccharidases have been applied to flax at various levels and compared to traditional retting methods. Pectinolytic enzymes secreted by soft-rot bacteria also cause maceration of woody fabrics that are long, strong and usually stiff. Pectinolytic and xylanolytic enzymes help in softening of these fibres. The combined alkali and enzyme treatment improves fibre quality.

Experimental

Keeping in view of the increasing requirement of the natural fibres for making handmade paper and the need of ecologically compatible procedures for producing such fibres in a consistent and cost-effective way, studies on bioretting of a variety of ligno-cellulosic raw materials (that could be of potential use in handmade paper industry) were carried out at the institute. This included the bast fibres like Bhimal, Paper Mulberry, Ankara etc.

1. Bhimal Beol *(Grewia oppositifolia Roxb.)*: It is grown and available abundantly in the state of J&K, Himachal and Uttranchal. It is a moderat-sized tree occurring upto 1700 m height. The tree grows upto a height of 45 ft. with 4.5 ft. girth. The barks of yield fibre used for making ropes, cordages, brushes etc. Its young leaves and twigs are lopped for fodder. However, its use for making paper has not been reported in literature. KNHPI, while working on the identification of alternate suitable raw material for handmade papermaking, could identify bhimal as one of the potential ligno-cellulosic raw material for handmade papermaking.

Keeping in view of its abundant availability and potential usage for handmade papermaking, potential of the bioretting process was explored for extracting bast fibre so as to make the process easier, highly productive and less polluting while improving the quality of fibre. For this, both the whole bhimal and bhimal bark were subjected to the enzyme treatment so as to extract bast fibre. First, whole Bhimal was treated to peel out the bark and then the peeled bark was treated to extract bast fibre. Simultaneously, both the bark and whole Bhimal were processed in conventional way also *i.e.* kept submerged in water for a period of two to four weeks so as to compare the benefits of enzymatic retting process over the conventional process.

Fibre Yield Obtained

The yield of fibre obtained after enzymatic retting process of bhimal was found to be improved by more than 40 per cent with improved properties of the paper in terms of strength and brightness. Besides to this, brightness of the pulp obtained from the APP of the bioretted Bhimal fibre was found to be 75.6 per cent ISO as compared to 69.8 per cent ISO, which was obtained from the pulp prepared by APP of the Bhimal fibre obtained through conventional process.

Comparison of the Commercial and Indigenously Produced Pectinase Enzyme

Besides the commercially available pectinase enzyme sample, one sample of the indigenously produced pectinase was also evaluated for its bioretting potential of the Bhimal bark and whole Bhimal. This time, the same retting liquor was used twice to see its effect on fibre extraction. First the whole Bhimal was put into the retting liquor and then the same liquor was used to extract fibre from the bark peeled out from the whole Bhimal.

It was observed that the same retting liquor when used twice was found to be as effective as the fresh liquor used because the amount of fibre extracted from the bark and whole Bhimal was almost equivalent in both the cases. Besides, the enzyme produced indigenously showed a slightly better response in terms of fibre yield as compared to the commercially available enzyme.

Comparison of Fibre Yield of Bhimal

Parameters	*Whole Bhimal (Conventional process)*	*Whole Bhimal (Bioretted)*	*Bhimal Bark (From conventional retting process)*	*Bhimal Bark (Bioretting process)*
Fibre yield,%	20	30	40	53

Comparison of Fibre Yield of Bhimal with Commercial and Indigenous Enzyme

Parameters	*Commercial Enzyme*	*Indigenous Enzyme*
Fibre Yield,%	18% of Wood 56% of Bark	29% of Wood 60% of Bark

Thus, it was found that the enzymatic route is giving a higher yield of fibre (about 1.5 times) while reducing the time period required to extract fibre *i.e.* from a long period of about 15-20 days to merely one day. Besides, it was found to be easier also for peeling out the bark or extracting fibre after the enzyme treatment as compared to the conventional process.

2. *Calotropis Procera* (Ankara Fibre): It is a plant 2-3 meters in height, blossoming white, pale or purple flowers. It is widely distributed in tropical Asia, Africa, Persia, Arabia and Afghanistan. In India, its main concentration is in the hot and desert parts of Rajasthan, Gujarat, Punjab and Bihar. Rajasthan is on the top of the list as it is available throughout Rajasthan but the heaviest concentration is in West Rajasthan-Bikaner, Jodhpur, Pali, Jhunjhunu and Jaiselmer. It is a calcarious plant and grows in sandy soil. The plant at present has no economic value rather menace and is yet to be fully exploited commercially. The bast of the plant yields white, silky, strong and durable fibres. It is reported that the tensile strength of this fibre is superior to that of cotton. The fibre is mainly used for making ropes. The fibre of the plant is so strong that people in Sindh and Gujarat in 19th century started marketing the tugs made from this fibre in the name of Manila rope (Rope made from *Musa textiles*) for tugging in ships.

Extensive studies carried out in the institute on bioretting of Ankara fibre have shown that a good quality of Ankara fibre can be extracted from the wildly available plants with just an overnight treatment of enzymes at ambient temperatures.

Fibre Yield: It was found that the enzymatic treatment of the whole twigs of Ankara could result into a yield of 20-35 per cent of the whole twigs as compared to the 15-30 per cent of whole twigs in the case of control twigs of Ankara. The higher yield could be obtained in the case of control only when it was incubated for a long period of about 10-15 days while the bioretting process requires an incubation of 1-2 days only. Besides, lot of biofilm also developed during longer incubation, thereby causing the problem of smell and water pollution.

3. Paper Mulberry (*Brousentia papyrifera*): It is a shrub or moderate sized tree. Its bark looks dark grayish brown/ greenish. It is extensively cultivated in the hilly areas of Himalayas upto an altitude of 3300 meters. It is grown at an extensive scale in various parts of India particularly in Uttranchal, Karnataka, West Bengal, Jammu and Kashmir, Andhra Pradesh and Tamil Nadu .

Previous studies at KNHPI have reported that paper mulberry is a good source of ligno-cellulosic raw material for making high-quality handmade papers. At present, the bast fibre is extracted conventionally by retting or by boiling the peeled bark in water added with a few amount of NaOH. It takes a good amount of time for cleaning the bast thoroughly. Therefore, the potential of bioretting was explored to extract a good quality bast fibre from the paper mulberry bark.

Fibre Yield Obtained

The yield of bast fibre obtained from the bioretted bark of paper mulberry was found to increase with the increasing dose of enzyme to a maximum of 57 per cent with the optimum dose as compared to the 50 per cent of the yield obtained from the conventional process. The pulp obtained from the bioretted fibre was found to be much better in terms of the brightness and strength properties than that obtained from the fibre obtained through conventional process.

4. ***Daphne papyracea*** **(Lokta fibre):** It is a deciduous shrub growing to the height of one meter and diameter of average 3 cm at the base. The tree is harvested after 2-3 years from the time of seeding. It is abundantly available in the North-Eastern region of the country including the hilly regions of Darjeeling, Sikkim etc.

Daphne belongs to one of the wild species of no economic importance and considered as wild weed. It is considered to be one of the potential raw materials for handmade paper making and is commonly used in the countries like Nepal.

Presently, freshly cut shoots are cut into pieces of 1 m length and packed in the form of bundles and for 1.5 to 2.0 hrs in water for extracting the bast with the help of hammering action of mallet and peeling out the fibre with scrapping tool. The bast fibre is then hung to dry. The cleaned fibre is about 15 per cent of the shoots taken initially. The extracted fibre is further treated with alkali to convert it into pulp for sheet making.

Preliminary studies carried out on enzymatic retting of the whole Daphne and the peeled bark have shown that the enzyme treatment results into a higher yield of fibre as compared to the conventional boiling process.

Fibre Yield Obtained: On having a look at the fibre yield of the enzymatically processed whole Daphne, it was found that 35 per cent of the fibre could be extracted from the whole Daphne as compared to the 25 per cent obtained on merely boiling it. While the fibre obtained from the treated bark was slightly less as compared to that obtained from the conventionally processed one (82% *vs.* 86%).

Comparison of Fibre Yield

Parameters	*Daphne Bark*		*Whole Daphne*	
	Control (Boiling)	*Treated (Bioretted)*	*Control (Boiling)*	*Treated (Bioretted)*
Fibre yield,%	86%	82%	25%	35%

Conclusion

From the present study, this can be concluded that the enzymatic retting or bioretting is a very simple process of fibre extraction that is equally effective in a wide range of bast fibres *i.e.* Bhimal, Ankara, Paper mulberry and Daphne. The process could be beneficial for extracting such fibres so as to make a good quality handmade paper because it has been observed that the paper made out of the extracted fibre is always better than the whole bark. The fibre extracted using the process of bioretting not only results in higher yield but also a better quality as compared to that obtained from the conventional procedures. The process is very simple as it operates under ambient conditions with an incubation period of 24 hrs. only as compared to the long incubation periods of 2-3 weeks being used conventionally. The process of bioretting might result into a reduction of the problem of water pollution also caused by the conventional retting procedures.

The process of bioretting thus developed might help in providing a sustainable and consistent supply of natural fibres to the handmade paper industry besides creating a good employment potential in the rural areas of the country.

21

Development of Speciality Papers for Archival Applications

R.K. JAIN, A.K. SHARMA, ATUL KUMAR and M.E. KHAN

Introduction

Most of the papers lack the durability and permanence that has characterized it's use since it's earliest application in recording the history of man and it's civilization. Although fundamental paper making techniques have changed little in nearly 2000 years, two innovation in the 19th century:

1. the use of alum as a component of size, and
2. the replacement of cotton fibre wood pulp are responsible for this predicament.

The sizing in the mass wherein rosin is precipitated on to the fibre by means of acid forming alum or aluminium sulphate into the pulping part of the mechanical paper manufacturing till 1980.Today a *p*H neutral and synthetic sizing agent is used. Cellulose from wood pulp is susceptiblė to this attack than linen or cotton fibre that is why handmade paper is found to have better permanence than machine made paper.

Handmade paper industry also adopted the use of conventional rosin sizing along with the addition of alum to fix thc rosin on fibre. With the use of rosin sizing, the paper becomes dull in physical appearance due to dark colour of rosin soap and there is a loss of permanence in the paper due to the acidic nature of the paper because of the paper suface interacting with the atmospheric carbon dioxide. In order to improve the permanence in handmade paper, there is a need to focus the attention of fibre reactive sizing in the handmade paper sector as well as the product according to the taste of valued buyer.

KNHPI has developed an acid free handmade paper and paper board employing various locally available cellulosic raw materials like banana, Sunn hemp, Daphne Paper Mulberry, etc. using environmentally friendly and ecologically compatible pulping and bleaching processes. The paper making process employed during production of handmade paper was neutral/ alkaline paper making thereby giving acid free paper and paper board suitable for preservation and conservation of old documents and manuscripts. The product thus developed will be an import substitute thereby saving the nation much needed the foreign exchange.

A survey of the handmade paper industry revealed that very few of the industrial units are conscious about the sizing process of paper since most of the industry are using acid sizing barring few of the unit and none of these are practicing the neutral sizing. There is therefore, need to develop to conduct detailed study to optimize the process condition for neutral/ alkaline sizing in handmade paper industry. In this area to develop techno-economic feasible process for production of acid free papers which would have a beneficial effect in terms of permanency and quality of handmade paper produced in the country.

Acid Free Paper Developed from Banana, Daphne, Paper Mulberry and Sunn Hemp

There is a thriving demand of acid free paper in the global vast expanding market. The reason behind this innovative change in the mind of buyer is due to high permanence value, more brightness, higher physical strength properties of the paper and resistance to acidic environmental pollution.

Continuously rising demand and cost of traditionally used cellulosic raw material like cotton rags and hosiery waste, being used in handmade paper making has forced the industry to look for the alternative raw materials for production of handmade paper and board. Search for an alternative and locally available lingo-cellulosic raw materials has been taken up as one of the thrust area of the research at the Institute for strengthening and sustainability of the Indian handmade paper sector.

Handmade banana, paper mulberry, daphne and sunn hemp paper can be best described as a revolutionary product which is much more sturdier than ordinary pulp paper and made from natural biodegradable product. This paper is popular among those who appreciate the concept of using a natural paper material in an original and organic way. A popular product that resembles one's ideology and sense of style, handmade banana paper is natural brown colour with natural fibres, made from waste banana tree which is cut after the banana have been ripened.

Known for it's strength (delicate and elegant look) this paper is suitable for a multiple usages like decorative, creative gift boxes, gift wrappers and handmade notebook, stationary paper and envelop paper. Banana paper has evolved as a superior substitute for mention 50 per cent of the current world paper and packaging usage.

Raw Material Scenario

Nearly 16.5 million tonnes/annum of banana was estimated to be produced against world production of nearly 36 million/ annum. Of the many varieties of bananas, only the cultivated and the edible banana are of economic importance. Available in Tamil Nadu, Kerala, Andhra Pradesh, Madhya Pradesh and Maharashtra.

Sunn Hemp is a annual shrub grown since pre-historic times and is second to jute as a source of bast fibre in India. It has now spread to many tropical countries where it is grown for fodder, green manure or as a fibre crop. At present Sunn Hemp is grown as a commercial fibre crop in India and to a lesser extent in Sri Lanka. Other major producing states are Bihar, Andhra Pradesh, Tamil Nadu and Madhya Pradesh.

Paper mulberry is available in the hilly region of Uttranchal and Himachal Pradesh.

Daphne is available in the hilly region of Arunachal Pradesh (Tawang District) and in the Tarai of Nepal.

Morphological and Chemical Composition of Fibres

Fibre Morphology

Characteristics	*Banana*	*Daphne*	*Paper Mulberry*	*Sunn Hemp*
Fibre length, mm	1.8 mm	3.12	2.83	8 mm
Fibre Dia, micron	23.00	20.20	30.00	31

Proximate Analysis

Characteristics	*Banana*	*Daphne*	*Paper Mulberry*	*Sunn Hemp*
Cold water solubility %	4.6	3.12	3.34	5.29
Hot water solubility %	8.1	4.90	5.33	9.6
Alcohol benzene solubility %	7.0	5.60	6.52	8.10
Lignin %	13	4.80	9.10	10
Holocellulose %	82.5	92.98	81.97	80.0
Ash %	2.25	3.10	6.52	0.61

Technology for Handmade Paper Making from Banana, Daphne, Paper Mulberry and Sunn Hemp Fibre

The exhaustive research and development work carried out at Kumarappa National Handmade Paper Institute has resulted in development of a suitable process and technology for making quality handmade paper/paper board from banana and these fibre. The technology all ready developed for utilization of banana fibre for making thin tissue paper of 8-10 GSM find huge potential for it's use in the domestic market like use in archival application for the preservation of old documents and manuscripts. This could prove to be an import substitute besides making a tissue paper. The institute also developed value added product like high GSM alkaline buffered boards for archival boards which find wide application for making products like storage boxes, containers, slip card and cartons. These boards of various GSM 200-1500 GSM were prepared after blending Sunn Hemp and Banana fibres. Since the banana fibre has it's own lustrous quality and inherent characteristics of shrinkage so blending is needed with sunn hemp to avoid shrinkage problems. The blending studies were carried out with buffering it with AKD and Ppt Calcium Carbonate to maintain alkanity as well to resist against moisture content and humidity when it is used in the archival purposes.

Adoptation of Eco-friendly Pulping

Among the pulping process tried Alkaline Peroxide Pulping Process was found to be the better process than the other processes.

Alkaline Peroxide Pulping

Pre-treatment with chelating agent

The raw material contains metal ions like iron, manganese etc. which if present may decompose hydrogen peroxide and form complex with hydrogen peroxide interfering the action of hydrogen peroxide so the removal of metal ions is accompanied with the help of chelating agents.

Chelating agents:

Ethylene Di-amine Tetra Acetic acid (EDTA)

Conditions

EDTA	=	0.05 %
*p*H	=	4 to 5
Time	=	30 minutes
Temperature	=	Room Temperature

After chelation the raw material is washed with de-mineralized water to avoid entrance of metallic ions through water. After washing the raw material is cooked with different doses of chemicals.

Conditions at Different Chemical Doses

S. No.	*Characteristics*	
1.	**Cooking conditions for all fibres**	
	NaOH	8 %
	Hydrogen Peroxide	2 %
	Time	3 hrs.
	Temperature	95°C
	Bath ratio	1:4
	Final freeness (CSF)	300 ml

Physical and Optical Strength Properties of Paper from Various Ligno-cellulosic Raw Material

Particulars	*Daphne 100%*	*Daphne 50% + Banana 50%*	*Paper Mul-berry 100%*	*Paper Mulb 50% + Daphne 50%*	*Sunn Hemp 100%*	*Sunn Hemp 50% + Banana 50%*	*Banana 100%*
AKD-2%Ppt. $CaCO_3$	Yes	Yes	Yes	Yes	Yes	Yes	Yes
Tensile Index (Nm/gm)	30.31	35.45	35.00	45.35	40.60	40.10	41.20
Tear Index (mN. m^2/gm)	15.80	16.80	14.89	15.06	16.00	15.50	15.86
Burst Index (kPa.m^2/gm)	3.00	2.93	3.13	3.83	4.50	4.93	5.66
Folding Indurence, No.	583	475	866	900	800	4500	5000
Brightness %	23.60	33.00	17.60	23.00	37.50	30.00	30.00
pH	7.50	7.20	7.30	7.50	7.50	7.30	7.20

Conclusion

From the results of strength properties it is evident that handmade paper from banana fibre is found to have excellent strength properties with folding endurance (5000) followed by paper mulberry, sunn hemp. This could prove to be one of the best fibre for blending with other bast fibres to produce quality handmade paper. Blending fibre with paper mulberry can provide paper of an opportunity to produced alkaline buffered paper with higher tensile required for mount paper for archival application .The studies thus could be for archival applications. The studies thus could be useful in production of various alkaline buffered handmade paper for fine quality like (tissue, mount and handmade paper and board) with better strength properties at cost effective price which could prove to be an substitute for imported paper by archival department. The process thus developed at KNHPI may be highly useful for Indian handmade paper industry.

22

Waste Waters for Handmade Paper Making

Preliminary Observations

SAAKSHY AGARWAL, A.K. SHARMA and R.K. JAIN

Introduction

Industrial environmental pollution is one of the major concerns all over the world. Handmade paper industry, as such is considered to be environment friendly, as the major raw material for handmade paper being cotton rags and the chemicals used for the production of handmade paper are mostly non-toxic. However, in the present day context, with application of technological innovations, increase in production of handmade paper, use of chemicals during the process especially when ligno-cellulosic raw materials other than cotton rags are used, the effluent from handmade paper units is loaded with more pollutants.[1] Even in the case of units using cotton hosiery waste, it has been observed that at times the effluent contained higher suspended solids, demanded more Biochemical Oxygen and Chemical Oxygen than the prescribed limits. To maintain the environment friendly credentials and sustainability of this industry, it is important to redress this problem.[2] Preliminary studies were conducted by collecting and analyzing the representative samples of the effluent from some of the industrial units. Findings of the studies are being reported here.

Standards for Small Paper Industry

Minimum National Standards[3] prescribed for small paper industries are recorded in Table 22.1.

Table 22.1: National Standards for Small Paper Industry

Parameters	*Discharge on to surface water*
*p*H	5.5 to 9.0
Suspended solids, ppm	100
BOD, ppm	30
COD, ppm	250

Process and Type of Effluent Generated by Handmade Paper Making

A process flow chart of handmade paper industry using cotton rags is given in Fig. 22.1. The points of effluent generation during the paper making process along with their nature are presented in Table 22.2.

Higher percentage of suspended solids was found to be present in the effluent from beater, paper making spillage and agitator wash. The suspended solids originating from these points are mainly fibres beaten to a certain freeness level. Efforts are therefore needed to recover these fibres.

Analysis and Treatment Studies of Effluent

Preliminary study was conducted on the samples collected from some handmade paper units. The samples of effluent of handmade paper units making various grades of paper were collected. It has been observed that at times effluent of these units showed pollution loads slightly above prescribed limits. This can be avoided by carrying out simple processes modification or simple chemical addition. Collected effluent samples were subjected to filtration followed by chemical treatment. It has been found that after filtration 50-60 per cent reduction in suspended solids, 20-30 per cent reduction in BOD,

50 per cent reduction in COD and 60-65 per cent reduction in colour of the effluent could be achieved. On coagulation of the filtered effluent with alum further reduction of 40-50 per cent in suspended solids, 30-35 per cent in BOD, 40-45 per cent in COD and 50 per cent colour could be effected. The final treated effluent was well with in the norms set by pollution control board.

Table 22.2: Process and Type of Effluent Generated by Handmade Paper Industry

Process	*Main constituents of effluent*	*% of Total Fibre/Fines Loss*
Potcher washer	Suspended solids having more fines	5.04
Wash of beater	Mainly having fibre as pulp locked in pockets of agitator	14.87
Agitator wash	Mainly having fibre as pulp locked in pockets of agitator	35.97
Paper making vat wash (Sanganeri vat or Autovat)	Having more fibres	38.17
Paper making spillage	Spillage having more fibres	3.78
Pressing	Pulp fibres	2.14
Miscellaneous	Solid waste of sorting and chopping process. Discharge of dyes and chemicals, coloured threads, plastics along with other materials having heavy metals like cadmium, chromium, manganese, zinc, lead and copper present in the waste. Heavy metals are contributed by dyes and binders in the waste cloth and paper.	—

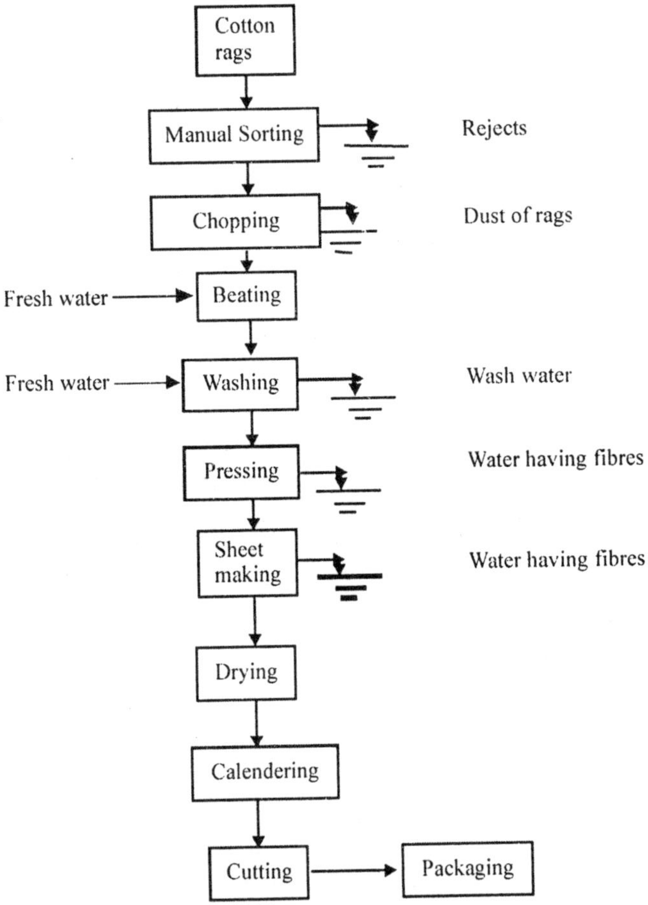

Fig. 22.1: Process Flow Chart Utilizing Cotton Rags as Raw Material

Study of Fibre Loss

The effluent of handmade paper units was analyzed for suspended solids and with the help of flow rate of effluent generated, the fibre loss was assessed which showed variation of 2.3 to 4.0 per cent. Simple filtration of effluent resulted in 50-60 per cent reclamation of fibres from effluent which could be reused. This could improve the productivity in addition to reducing the pollution. Further coagulation could result in 40 to 50 per cent fibre reclamation.

Water Consumption Studies

The quantity of effluent generated depends on the fresh water consumption in the process. Increased water usage also results in increased power consumption. The consumption of water by handmade paper industry ranges from 95 to 113 litres/kg. of paper. A flow chart of water usage is given in Fig. 22.2.'

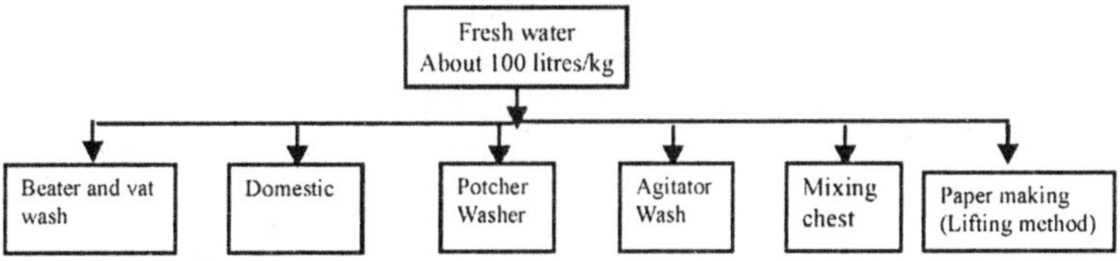

Fig. 22.2: Water Flow Chart

There appears to be good scope of reducing water consumption at various points by adopting simple measures, for example a study conducted revealed that on increasing the pulp consistency in beater (less water added in beater during beating) better strength properties of paper along with less power consumption per kg. of paper has been achieved. Therefore, there is need to conduct water audit of the handmade paper units in order to reduce overall consumption of water which would result in reduced power consumption and improved productivity.

Conclusion

Waste water/effluent generated in the handmade paper industry is generally discharged through a drain into the land, river etc. without any treatment. Some parameters which sometimes exceed prescribed limits of pollutants can be easily reduced by simple processes of filtration and coagulation. The effluent can be screened to retain fibre from the effluent by use of appropriate screens at the outlet of the final effluent. The effluent can be further treated with certain chemicals to satisfy the prescribed norms. Approximately 75 per cent reduction in fibre loss could be achieved with the simple treatment studies. The retained fibre can be recycled. The treated water can be recycled and used as back water in handmade paper manufacturing process. Handmade paper units on an average consume about 100 litre water per kg. of paper produced. The process modification by recycling the water can reduce the water consumption substantially. Possibility of recycling the water at some points of processes where fresh water is presently being used, needs to be explored. The possible points of recycled water usage are—Beater, Agitator wash etc. At several points fresh water can be replaced by recycled water. The closed white water system would minimize fresh water consumption; lowers fibre losses, fines and fillers. Detailed studies are being planned.

REFERENCES

1. TAPPI Test Methods.
2. American Standard Testing Methods.
3. Environmental Protection Rules(1986).

23

How to Setup New Handmade Paper Industry

PRAMOD GARG

To establish a new Handmade Paper Industry certain basic requirements have to be ensured as:

1. Availability of land
2. Availability of water
3. Drainage of water
4. Availability of electricity
5. Skilled, semi-skilled and unskilled labour.

Fund Requirements

Broadly the Handmade Paper units are categorized as tiny handmade paper unit, medium handmade paper unit and handmade paper unit with cylinder moulds. Funds are required according to the category of the unit at present Khadi and Village Industries Commission had scheme under which the finance can be arranged. According to the scheme the entrepreneur is required to arrange 10 per cent finance of the total project remaining 65 per cent will be arranged from bank/ financial institution, 25 per cent is given by Khadi and Village Industries Commission. In the case of S.C. and S.T. women, ex-servicemen, minorities, backward classes etc. the individual share is only 5 per cent. Khadi and Village Industries Commission contributes 30 per cent as grant; the interested person can approach State Office of KVIC/State Khadi Board.

The Nationalized bank and a few co-operative banks also have been approved by KVIC for the purpose under this scheme. The arrangements of funds is not difficult to establish Handmade paper unit.

Raw Material Requirement

Cotton rags are the basic raw material for the handmade paper. But tough efforts are being made to use other fibres as a raw material for handmade paper. Because the availability of the cotton rags is dwindling, the search is being conducted to find out the alternatively raw material, research conducted on banana fibre, paper mulberry and a few other agro fibres approved the potential of manufacturing handmade paper.

Tiny Handmade Paper Units

Any entrepreneur, who is interested to establish a tiny unit with a special purpose of manufacturing special high value paper, can establish a small unit at his home. It requires a small place of just 1000-2000 sq. feet.

Machines

One small beater approximately 5-10 kg. capacity with 2-3 H.P. single phase or 3 phase motor. The approximate cost of these machines would be Rs. 20,000-25,000.

Equipments

VAT
MOULD
SCREW PRESS
TAVSUKI

Man Power

About 4 to 5 skilled and unskilled workers will be sufficient to run a tiny unit.

Production

This tiny unit will be able to produce 10-5 kg. or 1-2 Ream Banana or similar Decal Edge Paper or 1-2 Ream small A4, A5 beautiful Decal Edge Paper per day for letter heads, envelopes or for other decorative uses.

Value

The approximate value of this product is Rs. 3000 to 5000.

Profit

The entrepreneur shall be able to earn Rs. 500 to 1000 per day.

If the entrepreneur starts manufacturing decorative papers and also convert in different value added gifts or handicraft items like carry bags, boxes, envelopes, lampshades, notebooks etc., this will give additional income to the entrepreneur. He can also engage the other members of the family to do the job.

Medium Handmade Paper Units

Those who are interested and have capacity to start a bigger unit they can go for medium size of handmade paper unit, this requires more people that means more employment more turn-over and more profit. The variety of production will also increase, the medium size handmade paper units will have the capacity of producing bigger number of wedding invitation cards, writing papers, fancy papers, file covers, cover paper etc. the quality of this product will also be a little better the medium size unit can produce up to 500 kg. of paper per day. If the unit is bigger, it is but natural that the machinery requirement will also be a little large. Approximately the following ingredients will be sufficient to established medium size.

1. **Water:** Approximately 2-3" bore water
2. **Land:** Approximately 1500-2000 sq. yards

3. **Building:** Approximately 5000-10000 sq. feet
4. **Rag Chopper:** For Cutting the cotton rags
5. **Machinery:** 1 or 2 beater—24 × 30 or 30 × 36 for pulping
6. **Screw Press:** For pressing
7. **Hydraulic Press:** For pressing
8. **Auto Vats:** For lifting the paper
9. **Calender Machine:** For calendering
10. **Cutting Machine:** For cutting the paper in required size
11. **Electricity:** 50H.P. approximately

Raw Material

The raw material requirement is almost the same as it is required for tiny unit but the medium size unit is better placed to have design development and research which enables the unit to use all types of fibre, blend it and have better basic raw material to produce better handmade paper.

The production of this unit will be approximately 500 kg. to 2000 kg. per day, depending upon the availability of raw material and labour input. The cost of this production will range from Rs. 50 per kg. to Rs. 80 per kg. overall profit of this unit can be worked out to 15 per cent to 20 per cent.

Value Added

With the help of little efforts entrepreneur start value added to his production, like making the carry bags, envelopes, boxes, tabletop gifts and various other gift items, with the help of little handwork, creativity, designing and workmanship.

Handmade Paper Cylinder Mould Units

The third category of the unit is handmade paper unit with the cylinder mould system in handmade paper was introduced in 1989. Khadi and Village Industries gave a new dimension to the handmade paper industry with the introduction of cylinder mould in 1989. The quality of the product has been improved with the quality input. Entrepreneurs interested to go in a bigger way for producing the handmade paper can plan to have a handmade paper unit with cylinder mould.

To establish the handmade paper unit with cylinder moulds requires following:

1. **Land:** 5000 to 10000 sq. yard
2. **Water:** 4"-6" Bore Water
3. **Building:** 10000 to 20000 sq.ft.
4. All machines as prescribed in "B category" Handmade Paper Units with additional 2-3 Beaters, 1 or 2 Cylinder Moulds, 8-10 Auto Vats and some other essential equipments.
5. Some units use Boilers, Digester or Solar Drier as per their requirement.

Raw Material

The raw material requirement is the same as it is for tiny and medium units.

Man Power

50 to 150 skilled and unskilled.

Electricity

100-200 H.P. with generator backup.

Conversion

Basically the sheets are produced by the handmade paper units that is one area, but it has great potential of diversification. Once the sheets are produced the entrepreneur with his skill can convert the sheet into the decorative item and these decorative items have no limit and any number of decorative items can be made out of the sheets produced by the handmade paper units. There are entrepreneurs who don't have their production units but they are only converters and earning more than what the owner's of handmade paper units are earning. These decorative items have great potential of export.

Export

India is one of the major countries who are exporting handmade paper and its products in other parts of the world. We have our name in the world market. Those who have knowledge and capacity can make in-roads in the export market through handmade paper. Khadi and Village Industries Commission facilitates the entrepreneurs to participate in the international exhibitions. There is a great potential of Handmade Paper in Export Market particularly U.S.A., Germany, U.K., Gulf, Italy, Australia etc. there is also big demand of paper products like Carry Bags, Stationary Items, Gift Boxes, Envelopes, Photo Frames, Note Books, Journals and so many various other items.

For Export Market the new entrepreneurs should create their website, visit or participate in different International Paper and Handicraft Exhibitions, study and procure the orders and execute the same.

Training

To start a new unit either of production or conversion, one must have training to do the job either he or she himself or herself should be trained or they should engage the trained persons to have quality product. Khadi and Village Industries Commission at different places like Pune, Jaipur etc. impart training to the probable entrepreneurs, those who are interested can approach the Director, Handmade Paper, Khadi and Village Industries Commission, Irla Road, Vile Parle, Mumbai, for getting training. One had short-term training can also think of having long-term training which will get him a certificate of training also. Infact the skill develops with experience but to begin with basic training is required.

Technical Assistance

To establish a successful handmade paper unit technical assistance is required. Khadi and Village Industries Commission, with State offices in every state, have a system to provide technical assistance to the entrepreneur. A National institute in the name of Kumarappa National Handmade Paper Institute, Sanganer is a premier institute to give technical training and also provide technical assistance to the needy persons. There are successful units which can also be used to get practical training.

Market

Indian Market

Now-a-days there is craze for handmade paper, people love to print their wedding cards, visiting cards, letter heads, souvenirs, meeting files, office stationery, paper bags, diaries, journals, photo albums, photo frames, Christmas stars etc.

Today a quality product has no dearth of market. There is a competition but there are virgin areas also, the only thing is the way the individual approaches but one should not feel shy for establishing the handmade paper unit only for the fear of marketing problem. There is national as well as international market for handmade paper.

Index